Praise for Rebels at Work

This lively, accessible book is full of practical wisdom for making sure that you don't become a rebel without a job.

— ADAM GRANT
Wharton professor and *New York Times* bestselling author of *Give and Take*

Rebels at Work is a brilliant guide for change activists who want to rock the boat and stay in it. As rebels at work we are too often marginalized and our great ideas go unheeded. Yet we are actually the salvation of our organizations. I love the fact that the authors are a living embodiment of what can happen when rebels get activated in a positive way. This book gives power to rebels at work everywhere. There are a few bosses out there who should be very scared!

— HELEN BEVAN
Chief Transformation Officer NHS IQ, National Health Service, England

Want to make change in the world? On GovLoop.com, we have 150,000+ government innovators pushing to make change in the often difficult work of bureaucracy. I can't wait to share Lois Kelly's and Carmen Medina's book *Rebels at Work* with our community. Their clear tips and strategies are essential to becoming a "Good Rebel" and making big change in big organizations. As a Rebel myself, I wish this book existed ten years ago, as it would have helped me avoid numerous pitfalls and accelerate success.

— STEVE RESSLER
Founder and President, GovLoop

Useful, practical advice and support for employees who want to think differently and find their own voice in the workplace.

— DAWN NOTT
Director, HR, Xamarin

Rebels at Work

Lois Kelly and Carmen Medina

O'REILLY®   Beijing · Cambridge · Farnham · Köln · Sebastopol · Tokyo

REBELS AT WORK

by Lois Kelly and Carmen Medina

Copyright © 2015 Lois Kelly and Carmen Medina. All rights reserved.

Printed in the United States of America.

Published by O'Reilly Media, Inc., 1005 Gravenstein Highway North, Sebastopol, CA 95472.

O'Reilly books may be purchased for educational, business, or sales promotional use. Online editions are also available for most titles (*http://safaribooksonline.com*). For more information, contact our corporate/institutional sales department: 800-998-9938 or *corporate@oreilly.com*.

Editors: Mary Treseler, Nicolas Lombardi, and Debra Cameron
Production Editor: Matthew Hacker
Copyeditor: Jasmine Kwityn
Proofreader: Eileen Cohen

Indexer: Ellen Troutman Zaig
Cover Designer: Mark Paglietti
Interior Designer: Monica Kamsvaag
Illustrator: Rebecca Demarest

November 2014:   First Edition

Revision History for the First Edition:

2014-10-29:   First release

See *http://oreilly.com/catalog/errata.csp?isbn=9781491903957* for release details.

The O'Reilly logo is a registered trademark of O'Reilly Media, Inc. *Rebels at Work*, the cover image, and related trade dress are trademarks of O'Reilly Media, Inc.

Many of the designations used by manufacturers and sellers to distinguish their products are claimed as trademarks. Where those designations appear in this book, and O'Reilly Media, Inc. was aware of a trademark claim, the designations have been printed in caps or initial caps.

While the publisher and the authors have used good faith efforts to ensure that the information and instructions contained in this work are accurate, the publisher and the authors disclaim all responsibility for errors or omissions, including without limitation responsibility for damages resulting from the use of or reliance on this work. Use of the information and instructions contained in this work is at your own risk. If any code samples or other technology this work contains or describes is subject to open source licenses or the intellectual property rights of others, it is your responsibility to ensure that your use thereof complies with such licenses and/or rights. .

All statements of fact, opinion, or analysis expressed are those of the author and do not reflect the official positions or views of the CIA or any other US Government agency. Nothing in the contents should be construed as asserting or implying US Government authentication of information or Agency endorsement of the author's views. This material has been reviewed by the CIA to prevent the disclosure of classified information.

ISBN: 978-1-491-90395-7
[LSI]

Contents

Preface

If you're reading this book, you're an idea person. When you see something that isn't right at work, your mind starts thinking about what *could* work. You want to make things better.

Maybe you've tried to get the powers that be to see the value of your ideas and haven't made as much progress as you'd like. Or worse, you've been told that you're rocking the boat too hard and your ideas aren't welcome, thank you very much. Talk about frustration, when all you're trying to do is make things better. "What am I doing wrong?" you wonder. "What does it take to change things around here? What can I do differently?"

Or, perhaps you are an idea person who has been reluctant to speak up at work because you're just not sure how to go about proposing a different way of doing things. You may be younger than most people, new to the organization, or have less formal education than your coworkers. You wonder how to be taken seriously and how to propose new approaches without jeopardizing your reputation or your job.

We used to be you. We struggled with the same questions and challenges. We made a lot of mistakes and learned the hard way about what it takes to introduce new ways of doing things at work, which is why we wrote this handbook. We wish someone had given us practical advice on how to create positive change early in our careers. "Imagine," we wondered, "what we might have been able to do if we had had a practical guide for changing things at work, a handbook with observations and advice about how to navigate the workplace and avoid common mistakes and traps."

Carmen worked at the US Central Intelligence Agency (CIA) and Lois worked for big companies and marketing agencies. While our careers couldn't have been more different, our observations of what it takes to be a successful change maker, or what we call a good rebel, have been remarkably similar. (See Chapter 1 for details on what we mean by "good rebels.")

Since we met at an innovation conference in 2010 and found we share a passion for helping good rebels inside all types of organizations, we have spent thousands of hours interviewing and writing about good rebels in all walks of work, from all over the world. All of their stories and advice, while distinct, are similar. Together, we share the following characteristics:

- We want to make things better at work.
- We believe the best ideas come from the people doing the work.
- We can't bear the thought of working at a job without possibilities for change and growth.
- We don't want to become angry or complacent or get thrown under the bus.
- We need and want help from other people like us.

Whom This Handbook Is For

We didn't write this book for managers, although we suspect many managers will find much that is useful in it. We wrote this book for the people doing the work, especially for those who care about doing their own jobs as best as they can and who want to help their organizations, companies, or government agencies do better as well.

Organizations being what they are, people often have to wage a minor insurgency to have their voices heard. That's one of the reasons we call ourselves (and others like us) rebels at work.

If you're one of the millions of people who are employees, we hope this handbook helps you become a positive force for change at work.

We don't want to suggest that we're somehow anti-management. Far from it. Both of us have had plenty of opportunities to manage and lead. But when we decided to write this book, we made a deliberate choice to focus on the challenges facing employees who want to improve their place of work and don't have the official authority, power, or influence to call the shots.

What's in This Handbook

This is the handbook we wish someone had given us. It's full of practical ideas, useful checklists, and valuable questions. It offers caring advice on what to do tactically, as well as how to manage yourself so that you grow and avoid burnout.

Here's a summary of the highlights in each chapter:

1. Good Rebels, Great Work	Good versus bad rebels	What change do rebels make?	In a world without rebels
2. What Makes Me a Good Rebel?	Born or made?	Rebel tendencies	Accidental rebels
3. Gaining Credibility	Understanding your boss	Developing your rebel alliance	Being trustworthy
4. Navigating the Organizational Landscape	Knowing how things work	Why people say no	Work politics
5. Communicating Your Ideas	What's at stake?	The vital 10%	Gauging reactions

6. Managing Conflict	Types & stages of conflict	Tactics for useful disagreements	Making controversy productive	Conflict, riot acts, anger

7. Dealing with Fear, Uncertainty, and Doubt	Minimizing the 10 most common rebel fears	Managing doubts so they don't manage you

8. A Guide to Rebel Self-Care	Heeding the warning signs	Retreat, reset, restore	When to let go	Finding the right boss

9. Am I Becoming a Bad Rebel?	The rebel arc	Avoiding bad rebel behavior	Bad rebel doing good

10. Give This Chapter to Your Boss	What motivates good rebels	Creating a safe work environment	Giving rebels the right work	Providing support and coaching

Afterword

Resources	Essential questions	Handy lists	Recommended reading	Glossary

How to Use This Handbook

There are a number of ways to approach this book:

Read and reference
> We invite you to read the chapters that appeal to you in the order that appeals to you, and encourage you to come back when you're about to shake things up at work again. Most of us have periods at work when things are going smoothly and our rebel skills aren't needed. But when you're about to take on a new challenge, please reread the especially relevant chapters before doing anything rash.

Start a rebel book club
> There are "Questions to Ponder" at the end of each chapter. You might consider reading this book with a group of like-minded rebels and discussing the questions after each chapter, particularly within the context of your own workplace. For the more ambitious, use the questions as a jumping-off point for a rebel training curriculum for your organization.

Join us
> Be part of the Rebels at Work community (*http://www.rebelsatwork.com*). You'll find good rebel profiles, additional resources, videos, a signup form for our newsletter, and frequent blog updates based on what we're hearing and learning. You can also join in the conversation on the Rebels at Work Facebook page (*https://www.facebook.com/RebelsatWork*) and on Twitter. We both use the @RebelsatWork handle, as well as our personal Twitter accounts. Lois is @LoisKelly, and Carmen is @milouness.

What You'll Learn

In reading this book, you'll find out how to:

- Achieve more success and less frustration
- Earn a reputation for having great ideas versus a reputation for being difficult
- Advance your career and avoid being sidelined (or thrown under the bus)
- Help your organization do more meaningful work

- Be authentically who you are versus trying to fit your work style to someone else's style
- Find more meaning and joy in your work

Will You Pay It Forward?

Figuring out how to create change differs in every work situation. There is no proven methodology that fits every situation. (If only.) If you find this book helpful, would you do us a favor?

Would you please reach out to other rebels and share what you're learning and offer some support, emotional and tactical? During our research, we have found that rebels at work are a generous, compassionate tribe, intent on making a difference and helping one another succeed and stay true to themselves in the process.

Together, let's write the next chapter about work where change makers are as vital to success as any technology or process or highly paid executive. Maybe even more so.

Not everyone in an organization needs to be a rebel, but every organization has and needs its rebels.

Adelante!

Conventions Used in This Book

The following typographical conventions are used in this book:

Note

This element signifies a tip, suggestion, or general note.

Warning

This element indicates a warning or caution.

Safari® Books Online

Safari Books Online is an on-demand digital library that delivers expert content in both book and video form from the world's leading authors in technology and business.

Technology professionals, software developers, web designers, and business and creative professionals use Safari Books Online as their primary resource for research, problem solving, learning, and certification training.

Safari Books Online offers a range of plans and pricing for enterprise, government, education, and individuals.

Members have access to thousands of books, training videos, and prepublication manuscripts in one fully searchable database from publishers like O'Reilly Media, Prentice Hall Professional, Addison-Wesley Professional, Microsoft Press, Sams, Que, Peachpit Press, Focal Press, Cisco Press, John Wiley & Sons, Syngress, Morgan Kaufmann, IBM Redbooks, Packt, Adobe Press, FT Press, Apress, Manning, New Riders, McGraw-Hill, Jones & Bartlett, Course Technology, and hundreds more. For more information about Safari Books Online, please visit us online.

How to Contact Us

Please address comments and questions concerning this book to the publisher:

O'Reilly Media, Inc.
1005 Gravenstein Highway North
Sebastopol, CA 95472
800-998-9938 (in the United States or Canada)
707-829-0515 (international or local)
707-829-0104 (fax)

We have a web page for this book, where we list errata, examples, and any additional information. You can access this page at *http://bit.ly/rebels_at_work*.

To comment or ask technical questions about this book, send email to *bookquestions@oreilly.com*.

For more information about our books, courses, conferences, and news, see our website at *http://www.oreilly.com*.

Find us on Facebook: *http://facebook.com/oreilly*
Follow us on Twitter: *http://twitter.com/oreillymedia*
Watch us on YouTube: *http://www.youtube.com/oreillymedia*

Acknowledgments

This book belongs to the many who have shared their stories, advice, and research, and who have been willing to listen to our ideas and help us make them better. Rebels are always learning, and so many have taught us so much during the process of writing this book, often in surprising ways.

Deep appreciation goes to editor Stuart Horwitz who got us to a first draft, and editor Deb Cameron who got to us to the finish line, and to those who read the first draft of the book and provided such honest, thoughtful suggestions, including Helen Bevan, Hugh Boyle, Maria DeCarvalho, J. Peter Donald, Christine Flanagan, and Janet Fitzpatrick-Wilks. Equally valuable were the reviewers who read the second draft: Cindy Alvarez, Curt Klun, Dawn Nott, Julie Soderland, Tiffany Wan, and Ayse Wiediger.

Thanks to all those who have shared their stories at RebelsatWork.com and to Peter Vander Auwera of Corporate Rebels United for being crazy enough to cohost a 24-hour online Rebel Jam with us.

A WORD FROM LOIS

I would like to give a big thank you to my amazing corporate clients who keep saying, "Yes, let's try it."

I am especially grateful to have married Greg Matta, who told me on our first date that he was a maverick and a feminist. Thirty years later, I treasure his kindness and encouragement to take more chances. That my sons Ian Matta and Greg Frishman are as supportive of me is a gift. That they are also rebels fills me with optimism.

A WORD FROM CARMEN

I want to thank my mother, Alicia, who went back to get her college degree in her mid-40s because that was the only way to get ahead at work. Her coworkers called her a pistol—another euphemism for a rebel at work.

I also want to acknowledge all the lessons I learned from my colleagues in my 32 years at the CIA. I want to thank the members of the Rebel Alliance—you know who are—and also the managers and mentors who guided and corrected me along the way. I didn't always follow your counsel, but I always appreciated it.

Good Rebels, Great Work

Good rebels just want to do great work.

We want to improve things that aren't working and that put our organizations at risk. Our motivation is not personal glory but introducing new ideas that can benefit our coworkers, customers, or community members. The greatest calling for rebels is helping our organizations evolve from what they are to what they can become, finding thoughtful ways to examine new ideas, identifying when and how to move on them, and taking the first step to get to a better place.

We realize the term "rebel" is loaded, so we'll explain what we mean. At the most basic level, good rebels are *for* creating new, better ways to do things, while bad rebels just rail *against* what isn't working. It's easy to complain but much harder to figure out what could be done differently.

A few years ago, we created a chart that shows the difference between good and bad rebels (see Table I-I). It has been downloaded more than 100,000 times and has shown up in tweets and presentations around the globe.

We believe it's popular for three reasons. First, it summarizes common behaviors of rebels. Second, it refutes the "troublemaker" label that managers sometimes slap on thoughtful people trying to make positive change. And, perhaps more complex, it shows that many who start off as good rebels get so disillusioned that they end up joining the dark side, even though they started with good intentions. The frustration of trying to get people at work to listen and agree to sensible new ideas can become so acute that good rebels can become pessimistic, point fingers, or become angry and obsessed.

One note about the chart: while it's useful, it can also oversimplify matters. Many of these attributes are on a continuum. At some point in your rebel journey, obsession with your idea may well be necessary, although we don't think obsessive behavior is a good long-term strategy for any rebel. To get management's attention, there may be times where vocalizing problems in public forums is more effective than slowly building agreement by socializing ideas with people individually.

Table 1-1. Bad rebels versus good rebels

Bad rebels	Good rebels
Complain	Create
Assertions	Questions
Me-focused	Mission-focused
Pessimist	Optimist
Anger	Passion
Energy-sapping	Energy-generating
Alienate	Attract
Problems	Possibilities
Vocalize problems	Socialize opportunities
Worry that…	Wonder if…
Point fingers	Pinpoint causes
Obsessed	Reluctant
Lecture	Listen

Who Are These Good Rebels?

Just who are these good rebels and what changes do they strive to make?

We've talked with hundreds of rebels over the past three years. They began their journeys when their concerns grew so acute that they felt compelled to act. Most would never consider themselves change agents, innovators, and certainly not heroes. They would, however, say they are people who care deeply about their organizations, coworkers, and people their diverse organizations serve, from customers and students to patients and citizens.

While some rebels make big, company-wide gestures, many more create small-scale changes. Here are some examples of rebels working in many contexts and roles:

- An administrative assistant, frustrated by coordinating meetings and decisions among vice presidents, invites other admins to a monthly brown bag lunch. They sit down to figure out better ways to manage their bosses' time and bring about organizational change from their sphere of influence.

- Exhausted by the layers of bureaucracy involved in approving innovation programs, a government manager sends a tweet asking the 1.35 million agency employees to pledge to do one small thing to improve the organization's effectiveness. Employees make 189,000 pledges on the first annual National Health Service (NHS) Change Day, unleashing creativity and improvement ideas throughout the United Kingdom.

- A 25-year-old communications manager, thrilled to be working for a law enforcement agency whose mission he greatly admires, sees new ways to use social media to help the agency fulfill its mission. When he raises new ideas, his bosses and the legal department cite complex and inane regulations. He wonders whether the government wants talent or obedience. He shows his bosses the risks of *not* adopting new ways of communicating and slowly gains support.

- A policy analyst shares ideas for improving the way a government agency carries out its mission. Her boss listens quietly but then advises, "Just keep your mouth shut and in 20 years you'll be in the position to make the changes you think are so important." The analyst resigns, convinced that no progress will be possible in her organization.

- After presenting an industry-changing technology idea to the executive team three years in a row, the sales director of a wastewater engineering company stops advocating for his idea internally. During the next six years, he continues to talk with clients and gather ideas to improve the concept. Ten years later, the company introduces the new system, which is a big success.

- A military officer rises through the ranks, modernizing approaches to leadership and professional development. He retires early, realizing that the top brass promote people with whom they feel comfortable. Those who rock the boat to create change don't make officials feel comfortable, and as a result, are unlikely to reach the highest ranks.

As rebels, our stories are different, but we have much in common. Table 1-2 shows some tactics and behaviors that successful rebels use and cultivate.

Table 1-2. Secrets of successful rebels

Tactics: Actions to achieve a specific end	Behaviors: How you conduct yourself, especially toward others
Tap into the brilliance of others, knowing that no one can create meaningful change alone.	Stay positive: optimism inspires others to join them in fixing problems.
Align ideas with the organization's goals. The more important an idea is to an organization the more likely it will be adopted.	Judge ideas, not people. Steer conversations away from personalities to focus on ideas and their merits.
Show how the benefits of change are commensurate with the costs of change.	Learn from anger: consider what triggers anger and avoid spiraling into emotional drama.
Use conflict productively: glean insights from disagreement and conflict to learn how to refine and advance an idea.	Respect others and consider different viewpoints.
Let ideas breathe, giving people time to absorb a new idea and consider its implications.	Know when to walk away, weighing the importance of the idea and the personal and professional costs of persevering.

In a World Without Rebels

For those who may doubt that rebels have a vital role to play in society, we invite you to reflect for a moment on what the world would look like without rebels.

We don't have to look far for examples.

We teach our children about the importance of free speech and the dangers of "groupthink," encouraging them to read novels like George Orwell's *1984*, in which the Ministry of Truth's real mission is to falsify historical events. Lois Lowry's *The Giver* portrays a world where pain, fear, intense love, and hatred have been eliminated. There's no prejudice because people all look and think the same. Yet evil lurks because people all look and think the same.

Nonetheless, in our schools and workplaces, groupthink is rewarded. Those who question decisions and advocate for different ways are often ignored, ostracized, or fired. (Two of our most popular blog posts relate to employees being thrown under the bus.[1])

Yet without rebels, our systems, companies, schools, churches, government agencies, and healthcare organizations become rigid and sometimes even dangerous.

---

[1]. See "Techniques for Throwing Corporate Rebels Under the Bus" (*http://bit.ly/throwing_rebels_under_bus*) and "When You're Thrown Under the Bus at Work: Part Two." (*http://bit.ly/throwing_employees_under_bus*)

Kids are teased, and sometimes bullied, for being different. Government managers obsess about protecting their budgets and headcount and lose sight of what citizens need. Companies don't see—or ignore—emerging trends and fail every day, putting people out of work.

The dangers of a world without rebels are often more specific, as well.

In 1986, engineers at the US National Aeronautics and Space Administration (NASA) warned that critical components in the Space Shuttle Challenger had a potentially fatal flaw and would not function well in cold temperatures. On a cold January morning, NASA officials decided not to heed the engineers' concerns and approved the launch. Within 73 seconds of takeoff, Challenger broke apart, killing its seven crewmembers, while an estimated 17 percent of Americans watched on television. A subsequent investigative commission appointed by then President Ronald Reagan found that NASA's organizational culture and decision-making processes greatly contributed to the catastrophe. The good rebel voices had not been heeded.

Responding to the ignition switch crisis that led to the recall of millions of vehicles, General Motors (GM) CEO Mary Barra publicly stated that the company's corporate culture had helped suppress the voices of employees alarmed about safety issues. Speaking up at meetings was not safe. In 2014, the auto manufacturer admitted that it knew about an ignition switch safety issue for more than 10 years before it issued a recall. In the interim, at least 54 crashes occurred and up to 100 people died. As 2014 unfolded, General Motors issued 47 more recalls covering more than 20 *million* vehicles.

Rebels inside Eastman Kodak foresaw the demise of photographic film and created initiatives to get into digital photography. Kodak leaders, happy with the profits of film and the comfort of the familiar, did not provide sufficient support to these initiatives. Not only did thousands lose their jobs, but the heart of a once-vibrant community was torn apart.

How could this happen when people inside these organizations knew about the risks? Welcome to a world where rebels are shunned and authorities cling to the status quo, resulting in irrational decisions and unfortunate outcomes.

Following an internal investigation, GM CEO Mary Barra said, "The lack of action was a result of broad bureaucratic problems and the failure of individual employees in several departments to address a safety problem.... Repeatedly, individuals failed to disclose critical pieces of information that could have fundamentally changed the lives of those impacted by a faulty ignition switch."

GM is not alone, or again, you might not be reading this book. Resistance to change, clinging to the status quo, and bureaucracy are pervasive, despite the pace of change in the modern world.

ORGANIZATIONAL SILENCE: WE DON'T REALLY WANT YOUR IDEAS

New York University researchers Elizabeth Morrison and Frances Milliken refer to this phenomenon as a culture of "organizational silence." In their article, "Organizational Silence: A Barrier to Change and Development in a Pluralistic World" Morrison and Milliken show that although organizations may verbalize openness to new ideas, most organizational cultures send implicit and sometimes explicit signals to employees that they should remain silent about their concerns.

"Because managers may feel a particularly strong need to avoid embarrassment, and feelings of vulnerability or incompetence, they may tend to avoid information that suggests weakness or errors, or that challenges current courses of action. And it has been shown that when negative feedback comes from below rather than from above—from subordinates rather than bosses—it is seen as less accurate and legitimate, and as more threatening to one's power and credibility. Thus, a fear of, or resistance to, "bad news" or negative feedback can set into motion a set of organizational structures and practices that impede the upward communication of information," explain Morrison and Milliken.

While managers may suppress good ideas, so can all the work committees, governance councils, task forces, and peer-to-peer collaborative initiatives that are proliferating as decision making becomes more distributed and less top-down. The desire to incorporate everyone's views can suck the life out of good ideas. A once strong idea can become so watered down that it's not particularly valuable by the time it escapes the committee work. Even worse is when valuable ideas aren't launched in a timely way because the committee meetings stretch on for months and sometimes even years. A good idea whose time has passed is not such a good idea.

SOMEBODY DO SOMETHING

If our current workplaces were a novel, we might be tempted to stop reading. "Good grief! People's souls are being sucked dry, and no one seems to care. I can't take much more." As we tried to keep reading, we'd desperately hope someone would help turn things around. "Please, get in there and solve the problems that are staring everyone in the face. Somebody do *something*."

Fortunately, we don't live in a world without rebels. Rebels *are* in every organization, in all types of jobs, and are learning how to turn things around.

Every day, people at work reach the point where they say, "Enough." While every rebel's reason for stepping up differs, almost all start with the same uncomfortable realization: "I have to do something about this." A rebel with a cause has an important role at work. The rebel is the one who will step in and get the ball rolling, regardless of title, seniority, or experience.

Not everyone in an organization needs to be a rebel, nor will every rebel continually want to be involved in leading change efforts at work, but all organizations need rebels who have the courage, ideas, and gritty determination to make things better.

Questions to Ponder

- What attracted you to this book at this time?
- If you were more successful at creating change at work, how might your life change? How might your organization change?
- Think of someone you know who is good at getting new ideas adopted at work. Look at the characteristics of good versus bad rebels listed in Table 1-1 and think about how they apply to that person. What can you learn from him or her?
- What might be possible if there were fewer bureaucratic problems where you work? What is allowing that bureaucracy to fester?
- What practices of successful rebels do you do well? Which ones are important for you to learn more about as you read this book?
- When we learn with another person, we often learn more and become more committed to making changes. Who at work could you invite to read this book with you so that you can support one another in becoming more effective rebels at work? Is there a leadership book club?

2

What Makes Me a Rebel at Work?

Do you ever say...

- Are our assumptions about this right? What if we think about it from a different perspective?
- I disagree with how everyone's thinking about this issue.
- Let's try this. It might be a much better way to get things done.
- There's got to be a better way to do this.

Are you a person who...

- Is curious, paying attention to emerging trends and how they might affect your work?
- Names the elephant in the room and has ideas about how to get it out of the room?
- Steps in to take on gnarly tasks that require creative solutions?
- Has been told more than once by a boss to "give it a rest because that's not how we do things around here"?

If you answered "yes" to one or more of these questions, you may very well be a rebel at work. Rebels ask hard questions, don't take things at face value, and don't accept that things have to be the way they've always been. We are also often the ones who can see the future coming and pick up on subtle indicators of change before others do. Above all, we're people who want to create positive changes, not just whine about what's not working. We're an oddly optimistic bunch, believing in what's possible while many of our coworkers give up.

Good Rebel from Birth?

Many rebels were born that way. Think back to incidents from your childhood and early adult years. Were you a handful even then?

We've heard hundreds of origin stories from rebels at work, and most—though not all—knew they were different early on in life, strongly suggesting that there is something about being a rebel that is born not made.

Venture capitalist and former Bell Labs scientist Deb Mills Scofield remembers that when she was three, her father told her to stand in the corner and think about what she had done. "Apparently I told him he could tell me where to stand but he couldn't tell me what to think," she recounts.

Encouraged by his parents to think for himself, designer Phil Schlemme stood up to his teachers in elementary school. They said he talked too much, though they admitted that what he had to say was interesting and benefitted the class. When he was seven, teachers asked the students what they most wished for. Most kids drew pictures of dolls and footballs. Phil said he wanted peace between Iraq and Iran and drew a picture of the countries' two flags. Around this time, he also decided he shouldn't have to wear the school uniform. Though his parents supported his decision, they taught him about conciliation and pragmatism. "My parents and I agreed that though it was all right to stand up to authority and think for myself, it might be wise to wear the school uniform occasionally so as not to cause a stir," he explains.

Episcopal priest and executive coach Maria DeCarvalho's independent spirit came to the forefront when she represented her high school as a delegate to the Girls' State Convention, sponsored by the Veterans of Foreign Wars (VFW) Auxiliary. "I explained to my hosts that I would not sign the required pledge to salute the American flag. I was happy to salute the flag but not happy to submit to a requirement that I do so. It was ironic," she said. "At the end of the week, the wonderful —and I absolutely mean that—women of the VFW Auxiliary awarded me the Citizenship scholarship, which came to something like $100."

How I Knew I Was a Rebel

I first realized I was a rebel in junior high school. In art class, I would create magazines, writing stories and drawing pictures about songs from the Rolling Stones and other bands. I loved creating those little magazines and kids loved reading them. But my work deviated from the art teacher's assignments, and so I found myself regularly in detention writing, "Obedience to authority is essential to growth and development" thousands of times. The upside was that the detention teacher was herself a good rebel. I vividly remember her challenging my thinking about Catholic doctrine and why I accepted Church rules but not school rules. From that rebel teacher I began to learn critical thinking.

In high school, I learned how to rebel *for* change instead of against rules and assignments. I became the first student to sit on the town's school committee, changed the yearbook categories to be more inclusive and less cliquey, and convinced the local newspaper editor that students should write about students. Challenging assumptions early on helped me realize that I had the ability and responsibility to act when I thought things needed to be changed. It has shaped my life.

A Careful Rebel

When I was a junior in high school, I was asked to write for the underground newspaper. Although I agreed with many of the causes they were arguing for and several of the undergrounders were friends of mine, I pretty quickly said no. My analysis was that they were not going to last long enough to achieve anything, and so I didn't think it was worth the trouble I would get into. I was a calculating rebel.

It's amusing to us that our rebel stories are almost diametrically opposed. There's no one rebel type. Rebels come in a broad range; just look at us!

Rebels Along the Way

Being a rebel when you're young does not necessarily mean you will continue being a rebel as an adult. Nor does it mean that you won't emerge as a rebel later in life. For some of us, the appetite to question persists or reawakens at some point in our careers.

Matt Perez found out he was a rebel while serving as a platoon leader in the US Army. His senior officers didn't want a female member of his company to be deployed to the Persian Gulf during Operation Desert Shield. Matt lobbied for her to serve with her company.

"From their perspective, sending a lone woman to a war zone was disruptive and counterproductive. I argued that, according to Army doctrine, we train as we fight. The woman in question was a noncommissioned officer and had trained to do this job, with this unit, in combat. To leave her behind because of her gender was a copout in my opinion. I pushed for her to go, against the judgment of my superiors, and despite my fear that any harm that came to her would be on my conscience."

Matt's story also illustrates how emotionally draining it can be to stand up for the right thing.

Note

You aren't a rebel at work the first time you voice an opinion different from the prevailing orthodoxy of your organization. You become a rebel at work when you decide to *continue* speaking up despite the costs.

Three Common Rebel Tendencies

How we think determines how we act. In researching rebels, we have found that they think differently from most of their coworkers. Many good rebels:

Are future thinkers
Tend to be more energized by creating possibilities than achieving certainty.

Tend to work ahead
See emerging trends early. Think several steps ahead of most coworkers.

Are different
Come from a different background or culture, so bring different ways of thinking to the workplace.

BEING A FUTURE THINKER

To learn more about the thinking styles of rebels at work, we asked rebels to map their thinking styles using the MindTime® (*http://www.mindtime.com/*) behavioral mapping system.

We found that the majority of rebels are future thinkers. Rebels can't stop thinking about possibilities and imagining better alternatives. We're driven to change, look for opportunities, and like working with ideas.

MindTime assesses how people think, uncovers why they behave the way they do, and helps predict what they will do. MindTime uses a phenomenological framework—past, present, and future thinking—as a way to understand people. Three time-based patterns help explain your cognitive style:

- Past thinking wants as much data as possible and is concerned with accuracy and truth.
- Present thinking seeks to create stability, and therefore safety, by controlling events and outcomes.
- Future thinking sees possibilities and intuitively knows which are the most likely to be opportunities.

Figure 2-1 lists characteristics of the three thinking styles. Looking at MindTime's visualization of the results, we see significant clustering in the results (see Figure 2-2), showing that we rebels do, for the most part, think very much alike.

The rebels in this experiment were predominantly future thinkers, but they were not 100 percent future thinkers. Most rebels fell in the intersection of future, past, and present thinking. This means that while their predominant thinking style is future oriented, they also have past or present thinking styles as well, enabling them to bring a practical approach to solving present-day problems and draw on data and past experience to validate new ideas.

If you were an extreme future thinker, with little past or present thinking, you would likely get lost in possibilities and not be able to complete projects. Paradoxically, if the majority of the people in an organization are future thinkers, the organization might behave very creatively and energetically but actually move too slowly to succeed, spinning in ideas but lacking the practical skills to realize them. To get good work done, organizations need people with all three thinking styles.

	Past Thinking	Present Thinking	Future Thinking
Self esteem from	Validated thinking	Goals achieved	Celebrated ideas
Known for	Being informed	Resourcefulness	Ingenuity
Needs	Information, data to understand the meaning of things	Rules and structure to guide processes and organize things	Options and flexibility to imagine new outcomes
Driven to	Know	Organize	Change
Life appears	Rational	Ordered	Emergent
Lives	Cautiously	Practically	Spontaneously
World view	Measured	Practical	Big picture
Looks for	Meaning	Usefulness	Opportunities
Believes in	Truth	Harmony	Hope
Respects	Evolution	Status quo	Anarchy
Works best with	Data	Processes	Ideas
Guided by	Rationality	Practicality	Intuition

Figure 2-1. *Three thinking styles (Source: MindTime)*

We find this mapping system useful not only in understanding your own style, but also in understanding how people in your organization think so that you can present your rebel strategies in ways that appeal to decision makers' ways of thinking. (We address how to do this in Chapter 5.) If managers are predominantly past thinkers, you should present solid data and research to support your idea. For present thinkers, show how your idea can be practically accomplished and meet the organization's goals. And if you're talking to a group of future thinkers, it's all about possibilities and opportunities.

Even if you don't use MindTime, you can begin to understand how people think by listening to the language they use and the questions they ask. Do they ask for best practices, research data, and examples of what other organizations are doing? Do they say they're not comfortable making a decision without more analysis? They are probably past thinkers. Do they probe for details on how the project would be managed? Ask what type of resources it would take? What current fiscal year goals it would help accomplish? They are present thinkers.

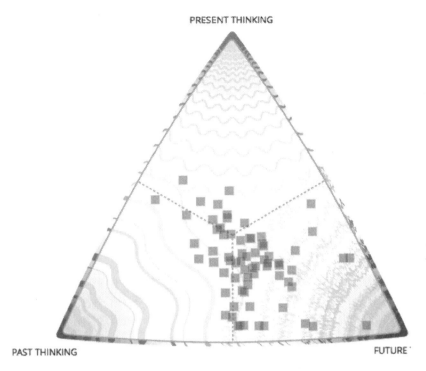

Figure 2-2. *Thinking profile of rebels at work*

This future-thinking trait may be why so many of us think way ahead of most of our colleagues, which can be both an asset and a frustration. It also relates to the next rebel characteristic: "working ahead."

WORKING AHEAD

In her article "Counseling Gifted Adults," counselor Paula Prober describes the early educational adventures of Susan, who was labeled as gifted. Susan recalled being thrilled about starting school but was very quickly disappointed. In second grade, she completed an entire reading workbook in one night. With pride, she showed it to her teacher the next day and was reprimanded for "working ahead."

While we may not have been labeled as gifted children, many of us were reprimanded at some point for "working ahead" and pushing new ideas too fast. We can't help it, or at least we can't control it until we become painfully aware of its impact on the workplace and on our careers.

Many of us see emerging trends and work ahead to figure out the essence of the trend and how our organizations can use it to their advantage. The challenge of working ahead is twofold: helping people understand and see the value of something so new, and not becoming bored by an important trend by the time the trend starts to be adopted.

But as rebels, we like living in the world of emerging possibilities. Executing the same types of processes and programs over and over again bores many of us.

In an online research study we conducted of 150 self-identified rebels at work, 94 percent said that "easily bored" is a very accurate (57 percent) or somewhat accurate (37 percent) description of rebels. Similarly, less than a third think rebels are patient. See Figure 2-3.

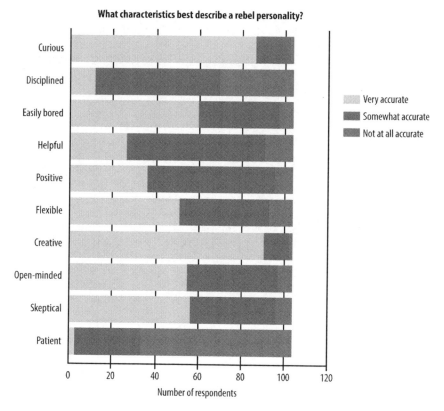

Figure 2-3. *Characteristics of a rebel personality*

Working ahead is what rebels do, but it must be balanced. Perseverance and tenacity are as necessary for creating change as seeing the opportunity.

BEING DIFFERENT

Because rebels think differently from most people at work, we are like any minority group inside a company. Companies often make space for people who are different as part of their diversity efforts, but they don't make space for their perspectives. In other words, if you were raised in a different culture, say Latin America, and you work in a Scandinavian company, you naturally bring different experiences and cultural perspectives based on your background. If your first career was in the military and you are now teaching in a charter school, you will have a different approach from teachers who never served in the military.

Differences are accentuated when you are also a member of a minority group. We have discovered that being a minority or a woman significantly increases the chances that you could be a rebel at work. In significant ways, women and minorities are often perceived as rebels at work, not fitting in and not understanding the corporate culture, even when they have no rebel intent. Their diverse backgrounds, unique experiences, and different cultural frames of reference contribute to them having different opinions and uncomfortable reactions to the status quo. It is sometimes overwhelming and confusing.

A Puerto Rican Woman in the CIA

 As a Puerto Rican, I was particularly sensitive to the issues that women and minorities had at the CIA and in the intelligence community. When I went to college campuses for recruiting and outreach events, I was often asked about what it was like being a woman and a minority at the Agency. I always gave the same answer, "Actually, neither of those were as much of an issue as just being a different kind of thinker. I often saw things differently from everyone else."

More recently, I have been reassessing that answer. As I was preparing my remarks for a Hispanic Heritage Month celebration, I realized that the answer I had given for so many years was a bit facile.

Perhaps I had it backward. It wasn't that being a different thinker was more of a career issue than being a woman or a minority. The truth was that much of what made me a different thinker was explicitly linked to my experiences as a Puerto Rican woman.

We suspect that many of you with diverse ethnic backgrounds view things differently from the majority culture at your place of work. Hopefully your organizations understand that people with different backgrounds bring different perspectives and ideas, and that this diversity of thinking is extremely valuable.

But we also know that many organizations value their corporate cultures above all else. In these organizations, you often hear a manager say things like "It's a shame about so-and-so. He has some interesting ideas but he doesn't quite know how to fit in." Or, "You have great potential but you need to learn to be more corporate."

Many sincere attempts to diversify organizations fail because leadership wants the appearance of diversity but not its impact. Any significant effort to bring diversity to your organization is tantamount to the injection of an important new way of thinking.

Note

Helping rebels be more effective at work is a diversity initiative. Increasing the impact of diversity on an organization is also a rebel initiative.

It's important for all minorities to understand that their organizations may not always be open and receptive to their ideas. To advance those ideas, they should feel free to borrow many of the tactics we recommend for rebels at work, even if they don't consider themselves rebels.

Accidental Rebels

"I didn't ask for this," you might be saying. Just as some people are naturally rebels because of their thinking styles and reactions to what's happening around them, others simply find themselves thrust into the role of being a rebel.

You might remember that one characteristic of good rebels we listed in Chapter 1 was reluctance. If you feel that way, it could be that you are an accidental rebel. It could also be that you are a rebel who has never wanted to see yourself that way.

Accidental rebels are drafted by their boss or by a cause relevant to their family or community. They may or may not have stories about being a rebel in elementary or high school, be future thinkers, or work ahead. They wind up taking on a role they never really wanted.

PATIENT-ADVOCATE REBELS

What if a health crisis hits and you're afraid your loved one is not getting the care he needs? Without any intention of becoming a rebel, you step up and become a patient advocate, a type of accidental rebel.

Pat Mastors was a TV news anchor and medical reporter for more than 20 years before her father was hospitalized. A hospital-acquired infection, *Clostridium difficile*, ruptured his intestines; he died six months later. Pat was called upon to be a patient-advocate rebel again three years later when her brother battled a rare cancer diagnosis, and when her mother had cancer surgery the following year.

But it wasn't until May 2013, when her 26-year-old daughter Jess developed symptoms of numbness and paralysis, that Pat fully understood the helplessness of having to rely on others to save someone you love and the need to go into full rebel mode in order to save your child's life.

Jess had hiked the entire Appalachian Trail the year before. Now she could barely move, stricken by Guillain-Barré Syndrome (*http://bit.ly/guillain-barre*), an autoimmune disease in which the body attacks myelin, the coating that protects the nerves. GBS strikes randomly and symptoms develop fast. Within days, her daughter could have been completely paralyzed.

Pat and her husband went into action, calling on every resource they had. Though they had confidence in Jess's medical team, Pat had learned too much as a patient advocate. Like all rebels, she knew that she must speak up, ask the tough questions, and be tenacious about getting answers and commitments from people who in many cases would like you to just go away and stop bothering them.

Despite the odds, Pat's daughter recovered. Did Pat's rebel actions make a difference? She'll never know. But she does know that people need to understand how to stand up to institutions and bureaucracy. To that end, Pat has recently published *Design to Survive*, a book that empowers people to be patient advocates.

CORPORATE SOCIAL RESPONSIBILITY REBELS

Sometimes the field you are in asks you to be a rebel at work. One example is corporate social responsibility (CSR), which requires organizations to create change and go against the way things have always been done.

Some people in CSR chose to work in the field and anticipated the challenges of getting companies to act with greater and greater commitment to societal needs. However, if you are drafted into a CSR role, you become, in effect, an accidental corporate rebel. You are asked to do something that may be foreign or unpopular in many areas of your company. Your job description may label you as the "champion" for CSR in your organization—a telltale sign, we believe, of an accidental rebel position. To succeed, you need to be both a good and an effective rebel.

These are just a couple of examples of accidental rebels. There are many more who find themselves taking up the rebel mantle by necessity.

Note

This ends the context about good rebels. If you're a possibility-oriented, work-ahead kind of rebel, we bet you're getting antsy, wanting to get to the guts of how to push the boundaries at work. This ends the overview about rebels.

All the following chapters dig into the "how to."

Questions to Ponder

- In what situation did you first realize you were a rebel? What did you learn about yourself?

- What rebel characteristics best describe you? Future thinker? Diverse outside thinker? Work-aheader? Something else?

- When you think about good rebels in your life, what makes them unique? What could you learn from them?

- What rebel in history do you most admire? What characteristics of that person would you most like to emulate?

3

Gaining Credibility

As a rebel, you need to gain as much credibility as possible so that people will listen to you. In fact, you want *so* much credibility that people look forward to hearing your ideas (at least once, anyway).

For that to happen, you'll need to work on three things:

Your relationship with your boss
Understanding management concerns

Your relationships with others
Finding your rebel alliance

Your own growth
Increasing your trustworthiness

Understanding Your Boss

It's almost impossible for rebels to gain credibility and trust if we don't understand how our bosses and managers think, what motivates them, and what concerns them. What would they like to be able to achieve? What obstacles do they face? What are they afraid of?

WHAT WORRIES YOUR BOSS?

Some bosses, entrenched in positions of authority, are suspicious of new ideas because those ideas might undermine their authority or, worse, diminish their relevance. For leaders in this situation, any kind of change proposal is immediately suspect. They are not thinking about whether the idea is good or bad. Their frame of reference centers on themselves. How will this idea affect my job, my status? Will I become less important with this change? Might I even become unnecessary?

Most bosses, however, want their colleagues and departments to be respected, grow in responsibility and resources, and thrive harmoniously.

While they may worry about the risks of change on a personal level ("What will happen to my reputation if we take a chance on this new idea and it fails?"), their real concerns tend to relate to risk and uncertainty, concepts that are all too easily confused.

Risk means you have some knowledge of what could go wrong. There are known factors to research and assess. The less complex the issue, the easier it is to understand the risks.

Uncertainty means what might happen is unknowable; you haven't done this before and don't know how it might turn out. The more innovative an approach, the more uncertainty there is likely to be.

One way to gain credibility with your boss and allay her fears is to separate risk from uncertainty:

- Be open about risks connected with your idea and describe how you plan to research and manage them.
- Be forthright about what is uncertain and unknowable, and what can be put in place to quickly respond and adapt as your idea is rolled out, thereby mitigating emerging risks.

What other worries might your boss have? Table 3-1 highlights some of the most common with suggestions for how to minimize them.

Table 3-1. Strategies for reducing boss's fears

Boss's worry	Rebel strategy
Worried about not having all the answers; wants to avoid criticism	Stay out of drama. Focus on the desired outcome, not the problem or its origins.
	Show how your idea supports management's agenda and objectives and makes your boss look smart.
	Help your boss present the idea to her boss.
Wants to avoid risk	Be sure you understand which risks most concern your boss. Talking about her concerns will help you be more effective and gain credibility.
	Determine whether your boss is confusing risk with uncertainty.
Wasting time and resources on something that might not work	Find data and research to support your proposal, even if it is anecdotal.
	Be clear about the challenges, which shows you've thought through the realities of making the idea work.
	Suggest an experiment to learn and test, with finite timeframes and metrics to gauge results.

R-E-S-P-E-C-T

Credible people treat one another with respect. While television shows like "The Office" depict the hilarity and sick pleasure of making fun of bosses, in real life, no good comes from doing so. We offer these suggestions:

Don't mock your boss.
Whatever you do, don't criticize your boss for being cowardly or too concerned about her own job security, because after all, that's only human. The fact that you both want job security may even be a good way to develop a common understanding. Neither of you wants to hurt your career. If you can establish that as a given, perhaps your boss can begin evaluating your ideas on their merit.

Warning

It bears repeating: never mock your bosses or talk negatively about them. It will *always* find its way back.

Don't go over your boss's head.
This can seem like the only option if your boss is recalcitrant, particularly if she forbids you to discuss your ideas any further. Going over your boss's head is like trying to draw to an inside straight in poker: the chances that it will turn out well are very slim and, when it doesn't work, you end up with the worst cards at the table. Once a rebel shows one member of a management team that he can't be trusted, he has almost certainly tarnished his reputation with every other boss in the organization. If you decide to do this anyway and it turns out badly, apologize sincerely and profusely. It's your only hope.

Don't worry about your boss stealing your idea.
We often hear rebels complain that management took their ideas and didn't give them enough credit. Our take? When a manager likes a rebel's idea enough to steal it, that's a rebel win. As rebels, we often have to swallow our pride and savor the internal satisfaction that comes from knowing that we planted the seed.

Note

Rebel win. When a manager likes a rebel's idea enough to steal it.

If it's any consolation, know that as a rebel you are likely to have new ideas, spot emerging trends, or figure out problems unimaginable today. Our creativity and vision form the pattern of our lives. They are a renewable resource we can depend on. Our creativity is our safety net.

LISTEN CLOSELY TO PICK UP IMPORTANT SIGNALS

Sometimes we lose credibility by continuing to push ideas our bosses don't care about. We keep talking, thinking we're educating our bosses while they just wish we would shut up. They can't believe that we're not astute enough to realize that they don't like what we're proposing.

By listening intently for clues about what bosses think about our ideas, we can ask questions, uncover their objections, and respond to them. Listening is the only way to get below the surface and find out what is really going on.

To gauge your boss's interest, listen to her language choices. Over the years, we've decoded some signals that tell us what executives really think (see Table 3-2; Table 3-3 gives free rein to our rebel fantasies).

Table 3-2. What managers say (and what they really mean)

What the manager says	What the manager really means
Does Jack know about this?	I want to be the one to present the idea to him because it's so damn good. Alternatively: this scares the hell out of me and I want to make sure Jack never hears about this.
I'll take this under advisement.	You're dismissed. If I approved this, I'd look like an ass.
Help me understand what you're suggesting.	This doesn't make any sense to me.
We need to get better aligned.	I want to see more compliance.
Have you talked with anyone in Legal?	This is risky on so many levels.
We have to keep the big picture in mind.	I don't see how this supports our goals.
Do you have industry best practices around this? What are our competitors doing?	This makes me nervous. (But if a competitor is on it, I may pay attention.)
I'm not sure your colleagues will like this.	I don't want to have to deal with dissent or disagreement in the organization.
Let's bring some people from other organizations into this.	Let's spread the risk. No way am I supporting this on my own.
I need to see more details on exactly how this would work.	I'm not convinced.
Let me be honest with you...	This scares the crap out of me.

What the manager says	What the manager really means
I appreciate all the work and thought you've put into this.	Forget about it.

Table 3-3. In our rebel dreams

What the manager says	What the manager really means
How fast could we get this done?	I love it. It's a slam dunk.
What else do you have on your plate?	I want you to be able to work on this and nothing else.
I'm going to review the department budgets this afternoon.	I'm going to move things around to make sure this gets funded.

Caroline, a product manager at an insurance company, was getting on her boss's nerves. Caroline knew that if a customer service rep got a potential customer to start an application for insurance, the customer was much more likely to buy a policy. Her idea: enter customer service reps in a sweepstakes every time they started a new customer application. She knew that the more applications that were started, the more revenues would increase. Caroline explained the financial expectations to her boss and her boss's boss, yet the idea stalled. When she stopped trying to sell her idea and dug into why it met with resistance, she found the problem.

Company policy said that customer service reps could not receive financial incentives for selling insurance. The company wanted to make sure that customer service reps were looking after the customer's needs, not selling policies for their own gain. With this knowledge, Caroline recast her idea. The sweepstakes rewarded reps only for *opening* and starting an application, not for selling policies. With that clarification, management approved the program, with great results.

Ask direct questions to find out what's going on. Saying, "I sense that this idea isn't a priority for you. What could I do to make it one?" can start a productive conversation.

Build a Rebel Alliance

You can't bring change alone. Nor do you want to.

The more we collaborate and learn from other people, the stronger our ideas will become. Chances are slim that any one person can identify the solution for a problem bedeviling a complex organization. Sharing ideas and inviting new ideas from others adds strength to your proposal. Listen carefully to what others say. If your ideas aren't convincing your colleagues, chances are slim that management will find them persuasive.

Further, the benefits of moral support are huge. We often underestimate how psychologically, emotionally, and physically taxing it can be to challenge the status quo. Our friends and colleagues not only increase our credibility; they give us strength, perspective, and sanity when we need it most.

An added bonus is that management takes us more seriously when we are plural, not singular. This seems obvious, yet sometimes organizing a group of like-minded people, from different areas of the organization, seems like too much work, and we try to go it alone.

So just how do you build a rebel alliance? There are many possibilities, from the informal to the more organized. Some ideas to consider:

- Invite interesting people, from inside and outside the organization, to have lunch on a regular basis to talk about your ideas and get their views.
- Set a regular time for a group of like-minded coworkers to discuss the topic. Maybe it's lunch together every Wednesday, a 30-minute conference call or Google Hangout on Friday afternoons, a weekly tweet chat, or Thursday night pizza and beer.
- Set up a community on your intranet or a private Facebook page where people can share ideas.
- Tweet and blog about your ideas, and follow people with similar interests to learn from them.
- Find and join an existing alliance, such as a LinkedIn group, a local chamber of commerce, or a professional association.

Surprising Alliances

 Be open-minded when recruiting people for your rebel alliance. I wouldn't have thought of "Grace" as an ally initially. Grace was strongly aligned with the organization, what many people would call a bureaucrat. Such folks aren't normally part of the rebel alliance. But Grace had mastered a particular set of skills—declassification and document handling—and had no other professional ambitions. Too in-

terested in my ideas about moving to the digital age, I didn't pay attention to Grace's advice at first. In fact, I assumed that Grace wouldn't understand my vision and would insist that things be done as they always had been.

I was wrong about Grace. She saw a great opportunity in the transition to the digital age. It gave her a chance to apply her knowledge and skills to an entirely new set of puzzles and she relished the idea. Grace became a great ally and not only came up with new ideas, but also warned me when an idea was problematic. This is an example of the benefits rebels can gain by casting their search for allies more broadly. In the case of Grace, she helped by alerting me to legitimate lines that could not be crossed.

Increasing Our Trustworthiness

Trustworthiness speaks to our character, but it is built through specific behaviors. Acting in a way that engenders trust is essential to being taken seriously at work, especially for rebels, whom some bosses don't see as team players.

Being trustworthy is not just important in the context of rebel ideas; it should motivate everything we do. We must be productive colleagues who can be counted on to honor our responsibilities. Too often we have observed rebels who forget they are at work and have a job to do. Nothing undercuts a rebel more quickly than letting her colleagues down.

Warning

We've encountered rebels who think that being a productive employee betrays their principles. They believe the organization is broken and any work on its behalf is wrong. We can't judge whether their view of the organization is correct, but it is counterproductive. If your dissatisfaction with your employer is so profound that you don't want to do any real work at all, then leave.

At its very core, building trust comes down to:

- Doing what you say you're going to do, whether that's achieving the sales forecast or completing projects on time.
- Being genuinely committed to helping your organization succeed.
- Helping others without expecting anything in return.
- Admitting mistakes and providing early warnings when you see that things are unlikely to go as planned.

- Not gossiping or saying hurtful things.
- Being respectful of others: getting to meetings on time, meeting deadlines, not exceeding the time allotted for you on the agenda, answering time-sensitive email promptly.

Dr. Linda Stroh has conducted extensive research on trust. She identifies 20 behaviors and characteristics that predict trustworthiness. Complete the self-questionnaire based on her work in Figure 3-1. What did you learn about yourself? Are there areas you could improve? In her book *Trust Rules: How to Tell the Good Guys from the Bad Guys at Work*, Dr. Stroh explains that the more people trust us, the more they let us experiment, take on projects that they might not entrust others with, and support us with senior management.

Questions to Ponder

- What's most important to your boss? What is she afraid of? What does she need to make decisions? What annoys her?
- What phrases signal that your boss doesn't care about an idea? How can reading these signals help you decide on the next step?
- Do you ask questions to clarify issues and have productive conversations? Is there someone at work you should be more direct with?
- Who are your greatest allies? Whom would you like to have as an ally? What is the next step in developing that relationship?
- What is the best way to create a rebel alliance around your interest areas?
- How trustworthy are you? Do you see areas for growth in trustworthiness?

Trait	Rating									
	1	2	3	4	5	6	7	8	9	10
Do you treat everyone the same, regardless of their level in the hierarchy?										
Do you admit and learn from mistakes?										
Do you demonstrate consistent good behaviors?										
Do you have positive qualities, other than good looks, a good education, and wealth?										
Do you never take advantage of others?										
Do you admit when you don't know something?										
Do you demonstrate absolute integrity?										
Do you genuinely consider others in your life?										
Do you voluntarily, in healthy ways, tell others when they are doing something wrong?										
Do you help others be better people?										
Would others introduce you to their trusted confidants?										
Are you likely to respond in a healthy way when you don't get your way?										
Do you hold yourself to the same standards you establish for others?										
Do you do the right thing?										
Do you stick by others in bad/tough times?										
Do you speak the same of people, whether they are in your presence or not?										
Are you likely to share resources?										
Do you have a history that demonstrates good values?										
Do you have self-awareness that demonstrates you know how your behavior affects others?										

Figure 3-1. *Trust rules self-questionnaire*

4

Navigating the Organizational Landscape

The more we understand how things work at work, the more likely we will figure out the best way to get support for our ideas and make them a reality. We can't change the culture and its associated politics and cultural norms. We can, however, learn the organizational environment well enough to navigate through it to increase our chances of success.

A common rebel mistake is getting so excited about an idea that we blurt it out to colleagues and maybe our bosses, and expect them to say, "Wow. Amazing. Let's make it happen." That rarely works, and sometimes backfires. In some organizational cultures, people who do this are labeled as "talking out of their ass" or "ass talkers." Not pretty or helpful to a rebel's credibility.

So before you share your ideas with others, spend as much time as you can learning the organizational landscape, as well as all the ways previous reform or innovation efforts failed.

In this chapter, we'll share ideas for learning:

- How things really work
- Why people say no
- Which relationships are especially important
- Behaviors that can help you sail around political and bureaucratic traps

How Do Things Really Work?

To be effective, we need to become students of the way the organization actually works (as opposed to the way we wish it might work or think it should work).

Especially important is knowing what the organization values (stated or unstated) and how decisions are made.

WHAT IS MOST VALUED?

People in organizations pay attention to what the organization most values. At its most basic, this is about understanding the essential elements of the organization's culture. To get at what's most valued, ask yourself questions like:

- Is this a mission-centric or customer-centric organization? Or is it a support organization that is most concerned with keeping the hierarchy around it happy and satisfied?
- What kinds of ideas do people pay attention to and what is usually dismissed?
- Has the organization endured a recent trauma that is leading everyone to play it safe, or alternatively, has a new leader taken over who is encouraging bold ideas?

What's most valued will guide you in positioning your ideas. Are customers most valued? If so, can you link your idea to customers in some way? Are ideas about administrative issues, such as parking, not valued? If so, is it worth your professional reputation to put a lot of effort into trying to change parking privileges? (Could you frame parking privileges as a customer issue? For example, happier employees will go the extra mile to help customers.) The more you can link with what the organization values, the more likely it is that your idea will be considered.

It's Not Easy Being Green

As part of a much larger creative project for a Melbourne hair products manufacturer, Phil Schlemme pointed out that the company was using 100 percent virgin plastics for all its packaging, which conflicted with the company's recently defined green initiatives. Here's Phil's story.

"On a Monday we held discussions about moving to recycled plastic (which uses 70 percent less energy in the manufacture). There was great resistance from within along the lines of 'too hard' and 'can't do it now, costs too much.' I pressed my point that it was a little incongruous to have newly defined vision, mission, and values only to reject movement toward a more sustainable future at the very first hurdle. A long conversation with the plastic bottle and tub manufacturer ensued and issues of supply and quality were raised.

"By Friday of that week, we had working samples and a provisional agreement for 100 percent recycled plastic pellets in the three plastics we needed and the change was made at no extra cost. The toolmaker was also consulted to thin the walls of the packaging without affecting structural performance, thus saving more plastic. One week to dramatically change the direction and performance of the company. Subsequently, we won Gold at the Australian Packaging Awards in the Export Category for our commitment to the environment and were recognized by Sustainability Victoria."

HOW ARE DECISIONS MADE?

Take a look at how decisions are made overall. Is the organization surprisingly democratic in its processes and does it value consensus? Or is there a strong executive who has the authority to make command decisions? Does it have many independent power centers or is there more of a traditional hierarchy? Who influences whom?

Knowing this helps determine the people with whom you need to build relationships. As you build those relationships, find out what's important to those people and their organizations. By doing so, you can connect your ideas to what's important to those decision makers. For example, if the steering committee that makes decisions about technology is intent on reducing complexity, show how your idea reduces complexity. If HR decision makers are looking to attract a younger demographic, show how your idea will appeal to millennials.

What are the business cycles?

What's the rhythm and pace of your organization? How long do executives typically serve in their positions? If you work in a government organization, which leadership positions are likely to be affected by a change in administration? Reform efforts can fail when their champions move on to other positions.

It is also important to learn how the money works. When do planning and budget meetings start for the next fiscal year? When is the plan and budget locked down? If planning meetings for the next fiscal year start in July, you probably want to present your idea by June at the latest to get into the July discussions. If you propose your idea in the fall, the chances of it being considered or funded may be minimal. Learn when and how to insert your idea into the timing of decisions, which varies in every organization.

How are resources allocated for new projects?

While you're following the money, pay special attention to how new ideas get funded. Sometimes an organization will have a structured approach to investing in new projects with a formal approval process. In our experience, this can be both good and bad for rebels. It's good in that the organization at least recognizes the need to refresh its processes on a regular basis, but bad because these innovation and new investment allocations can become political, with favored executives getting funded first at the expense of quality ideas.

You may find that your organization has not set aside a specific investment fund, in which case you will likely have to convince a program manager that your idea needs to be one of his goals. You may need to come up with a way of testing your idea that requires many fewer resources, which is hard! Our experience is that even ideas that don't appear to require new funding can have hidden costs. Even something as trivial as making a small change in a drop-down menu can end up as a line item on someone else's budget.

Why Do People Say No?

Mastering the organizational landscape also means finding out why people say no. Here are some tools you can use to explore where the resistance is coming from.

THE FIVE WHYS

The "five whys" is a useful approach for getting at cause-effect relationships behind problems or resistance to new ideas. A five-why analysis might proceed this way:

- Why does Ms. X oppose the idea? She thinks it's disruptive.
- Why does she think it's disruptive? It would mess with the sales process.
- Why does she think it would mess with the sales process? Because it would make it harder to keep metrics.
- Why does she think it would be harder to keep metrics? Because salespeople will be spending all their time on the new approach.
- Why would salespeople have to spend all their time? Because salespeople aren't good enough writers to prepare the consumer sentiment analysis you want.

By exploring at least five "why" questions in your analysis, you go deep enough to uncover the real implementation problems for your idea. (By the way, this technique was originally developed by Sakichi Toyoda (*http://bit.ly/sakichi_toyoda*) and was used within the Toyota Motor Corporation (*http://en.wikipedia.org/wiki/Toyota*) during the evolution of its manufacturing methodologies.)

WHAT'S THEIR PERSPECTIVE?

Another approach is perspective taking: the ability to see things from others' perspectives. Too many of us run into a dead end because we push ideas forward based on how *we* see the situation without stopping to consider the decision makers' viewpoints. Understanding what it's like to be them can give us clues to how to position our idea—or how likely the idea is to be considered. (This can save you a lot of angst and wasted energy.)

> ### Note
>
> Organizations are made up of people. All change affects people. You may have a strategy that could double sales, cut costs by a third, and win industry admiration. Nonetheless, it still affects people. To be successful, figure out how people feel and what anxieties or fears your idea might provoke, and then factor that into how you frame, socialize, and implement your idea.
>
> Organizations don't change; people do.
>
> "Leadership" doesn't say yay or nay to an idea; people do.

Which Relationships Are Especially Important?

The most important part of mastering the organizational landscape is understanding the different types of people who populate it and which relationships are especially important to build. Most of us tend to develop relationships with people we like and who are like us, and avoid people whose views and mind-sets are really different from our own.

But when it comes to creating change, we need to develop relationships with people who can help us or stop us. We're talking primarily about the people who fall into the category of bureaucrats.[1] They're pretty much everyone's favorite people to mock and disparage, but our advice is to invest your energy in better understanding the varying roles that bureaucrats play in organizations. We'll even go so

---

1. Bureaucrats are everywhere: in government, in large corporations, and even in small companies.

far as to suggest that befriending some of these bureaucrats could end up being one of the most useful things rebels can do to improve their chances for success.

WORK POLITICS: FOUR TYPES OF PEOPLE YOU MAY MEET

So, what exactly is a bureaucrat anyway? More than a century ago, Max Weber, one of the fathers of sociology, described a bureaucrat as a person who faithfully uses his judgment and skills in service of a higher authority and who "must sacrifice his personal judgment if it runs counter to his official duties."

Based on our experience in government and business, we think Weber's definition is not adequately nuanced. Some bureaucrats are interested in nudging the organization in the right direction, while others are more concerned with completing their to-do lists on time and on budget or even—gasp—advancing their own careers.

Here are four of the most noteworthy types of bureaucrats you'll encounter (see Figure 4-1).

Bureaucratic black belts

We use the term bureaucratic black belts (BBBs) to describe people who have mastered their organization's rules and culture and whose primary motivations appear to be making sure that the organization's rules are followed and operational integrity is maintained.

If you recall the thinking styles discussed in Chapter 2, BBBs are likely to be strong present thinkers, more motivated by getting things done than by imagining how they could be done better. BBBs are pros at making all sorts of things happen by leveraging the organization's existing regulations. BBBs hold all kinds of positions, though you will find them most in areas such as legal, finance, HR, customer service, quality management, compliance, and sustainability. If a person's job involves any sort of regulatory, compliance, product quality, or public-reputation risks, that person is more likely to be a BBB to some degree. Such workers have to be, really. Their responsibility is to make sure things go as planned and to protect the organization from disruptive surprises.

BBBs can be anywhere. We've met presidents of ad agencies, heads of sales, leaders of government departments, CEOs, and even heads of innovation strategy who were full-fledged BBBs. Micromanagers are BBBs extraordinaire.

BBBs may consider our creative, intuitive thinking style as flighty, not grounded in what's needed to run the organization. As defenders of the integrity of the process, they are rightfully and responsibly concerned that the turbulence of a new idea might upset important procedures and norms. This may make them suspicious and skeptical of a rebel's ideas from the get-go.

Tugboat pilots

Tugboat pilots are often some of the most valuable members of an organization's leadership team because of their ability to navigate difficult organizational terrain, whether congressional hearings, new leadership, bad publicity, or new administrations. Like mountain goats, their first step, their first bureaucratic response, is always spot-on. They can recall every detail of an organization's history and leverage it to their advantage.

They differ from BBBs in that their orientation is not conservative, per se. They are motivated not so much by making sure the organization's rules are followed as by figuring out the best way to get the organization's mission accomplished. They are much less likely than rebels to imagine significant new approaches, because they value expediency, sound tactics, and near-term results.

Tugboat pilots are masters of context and of reading people. They seem to have recognized early in their careers that their innate skills are suited to guiding others and embrace that mission with enthusiasm. You sometimes see a very experienced tugboat pilot who has been the righthand person of a senior leader for many years. The senior leader is likely to be dynamic and hard-charging and perhaps was once a rebel, and their symbiotic relationship is quite productive. The tugboat pilot is the person who helps turn the leader's often instinctive insights into policies and processes the rest of the organization can implement.

Because of these characteristics, a relationship with a tugboat pilot can be invaluable to a rebel. Unfortunately, they don't wear nametags identifying themselves, so we need to do some homework to spot them.

One approach is to talk with people like chiefs of staff and executive assistants. These people can help you identify the tugboat pilots. (They might even end up being the tugboat pilots themselves.) When you connect with tugboat pilots, ask them open-ended questions, such as what makes for a good meeting in the organization or how senior leaders like to receive information. Tugboat pilots pride themselves on holding crisp meetings, so seek their advice before presenting your ideas.

But beware—the instincts of tugboat pilots are likely more conservative than yours. Taking a chance in dangerous waters is just not their style.

Benevolent bureaucrats

Benevolent bureaucrats can slow your progress down, but not because they want to stop you. These kinder, gentler bureaucrats may calculate that your change idea has a chance of winning support from senior leaders, and they want to be associated with the Big Deal in some way. They don't know enough about your initiative to provide substantive value, so they pick on small things.

For example, HR may step in and say that to succeed you should use its new interactive training methodology and world-class learning platform. Or the former journalist in the marketing department may nitpick language describing the initiative. "Is this really the right word to describe what you're trying to achieve?" Or the IT people want more meetings to discuss how to establish baseline analytics so that the program measurement will be as accurate as possible.

Before long, you find yourself stuck in a multitude of bureaucratic meetings that can slow project progress to a crawl.

What to do?

Ask the benevolent bureaucrats to give you their recommendations in writing by a certain date (the sooner the better so that you can stay on track and focus on the most important next steps for advancing your initiative). Often they'll miss the deadline.

Thank them for their ideas and tell them you'll circle back to them when you think the timing is right to focus on training or wordsmithing or analytics.

By all means, keep going. Don't let the benevolent bureaucrats' desire to be somehow involved slow you down.

Your success is about achieving results important to your organization. Going to unnecessary meetings with nice people whose ideas aren't especially relevant slows down results and success.

Wind surfers

Wind surfers are one of the most difficult personality types rebels will find in the organizational landscape. Wind surfers are BBBs with strong personal ambitions who have mastered the organizational landscape—and every angle to ascend the hierarchy. While they may have held convictions about how the organization could improve early in their careers, over time and usually without conscious awareness, their ambitions overcome their desire to improve the organization's effectiveness.

Of course, they would deny this and insist they are just playing for the right time and opportunity, but the opportunity never seems to come. And in the meantime, their views on what the organization needs to do shift with the prevailing winds of leadership.

The organizational astuteness of wind surfers is prized by more adventurous leaders, who can often use their support to get their own initiatives implemented. Wind surfers are always happy to do the bidding of those above them in the hierarchy but are reluctant to back ideas that come from below. This is why we think rebels should approach such personalities with great caution. You are unlikely to gain a hearing from them. If you do, know that their primary motivation will be to explore how your idea can help them. You might still be able to use their assistance, but do not expect wind surfers to have your back if the rest of the organization begins to resist your ideas.

Organizational native	What they care about	What they know	Potential as an ally
Bureaucratic black belt	Rules	Secrets and traditions of the organization	Give it a try - medium
Tugboat pilot	Results	How things get done	Highest—Can become a valuable resource
Benevolent bureaucrat	Process	Details, details, details	Low
Wind surfer	Themselves	How to get ahead	Really low

Figure 4-1. *Types of bureaucrats*

There are many types of people in the workplace, and it is not our intention to pigeonhole them. On the other hand, we want to share common behaviors of bureaucrats whom we have known as rebels at work. The more we know how things —and people—tend to work, the better the relationships we can develop. From now on, we'll refer to bureaucrats collectively as BBBs unless there's a good reason to call out one particular type of bureaucrat.

DEVELOPING GOOD RELATIONSHIPS

Is your idea especially important to the organization right now? Do you think it could make a difference? If so, make friends with those individuals in the organization who can help you make it happen. Remember, most people don't see as far ahead as we do or make the intuitive leaps in connecting how an idea will have a positive ripple effect. They need us to slow down and communicate in ways that make sense to them.

A good first step is getting to know people as people and giving them an opportunity to get to know you. We ask people who take our courses to do this, and they say it is one of the most helpful things that they have done at work in quite a while. Set up lunch dates with BBBs so that you can begin to understand them. In these informal relationship-development conversations, try to learn what it's like to be them. Put yourself in their place:

- What are they accountable for?
- What are their motivations?
- What does success look like to them?
- What happens if they make a mistake?

Respect other views

As unlikely as it may seem, BBBs and many others in your organization may actually love the way things are and believe the status quo is just as it should be. One of the greatest mistakes rebels can make is failing to understand that many leaders want to preserve what they have because they genuinely believe in it.

Those who oppose ideas for change aren't stupid or acting only out of self-interest. For many, the changes we advocate strike at the very essence of something they believe in deeply. Understanding this will impact your approach. You are less likely to underestimate those who don't support you and much more willing to engage in real conservations with them to identify areas for synergy.

The Company I Almost Bought

One of my favorite jobs was building a public relations division of a respected advertising agency. Our young team did remarkable work, bringing in new clients, developing creative approaches to our profession, attracting national talent, and growing revenue at a faster rate than the advertising side of the business. We felt unstoppable.

Our band of rebels also felt frustrated with the agency's conservative ownership. So it was thrilling when I started talking with the owners about ways to buy out their ownership. Imagine, I thought, what we could do without these kind yet obstructive benevolent bureaucrats controlling the company.

When we discussed terms of the deal, I was frank about what I thought needed to change. There were too many people working on the advertising side of the business who had not kept up with industry trends and who accepted good enough as good enough. That would have to change. Our business couldn't grow if we had all this old-thinking baggage.

What I failed to realize is how much the owners valued the loyalty of their long-time employees. To them, loyalty meant more than creativity, even though we were selling creativity. While I was talking about possibilities and change, they talked about stability and job security.

Negotiations broke off, and I left to take another position, reluctantly leaving one of the best teams I had ever worked with. If I had tuned into the owners' perspectives, I may have been able to position my ideas in ways that scared them less. I could have acknowledged their concerns for their employees and discussed ways to help those people develop. But, as many rebels do, I spent more time thinking about ideas for what the agency could become and not enough time developing relationships with the owners so that they would be comfortable allowing me to implement those ideas.

Empathize: What's it like to be them?

Developing genuine empathy for those in the organization with bureaucratic tendencies is foundational for building relationships. Tune into their anxieties. We know this can be challenging, especially if you've been continually foiled by BBBs, but it's essential to getting to know them.

Bring this empathy to your conversations, letting people know that you want to understand their perspective. All people want to be seen and to have people understand what it's like to be them. This is especially true of BBBs, who may have an even more difficult role at work than rebels do. Empathy is likely to ease the tension and will perhaps put BBBs slightly more at ease with you.

Developing these relationships is in essence a negotiating step, and empathy is one of the five core skills in negotiating, according to Robert Fisher and Samuel Williston of the Harvard Negotiation Project. The other four, which are also useful for rebels, are:

- Making people feel personally connected to you
- Showing how the idea preserves or expands the other person's autonomy

- Acknowledging the other person's status
- Making people feel that they have a say and are playing a meaningful role in the negotiations

This may feel like "sucking up." It is not. It is acknowledging the humanity of each of us and connecting on that level. Kindness is an incredibly powerful tool for creating relationships and positive change at work.

Ways to Avoid Organizational Traps

Understanding the environment you're working in is half the battle; the other half is managing your own enthusiasm about your idea and vision. Here are some effective behaviors to adopt.

DON'T IMPROVISE

It's important not to wing it when going into meetings. Have a goal in mind whenever you have a conversation. What do you want people to do, or not to do, after the conversation happens? The more clear and precise your goal, the more likely you'll achieve it.

Free-flowing, unstructured conversations can be dangerous because we tend to get passionate and excited about what's possible. Passionate possibilities send warning signals to bureaucrats concerned more about order. "Danger! Danger! This person is not staying inside the lines; he is even talking about painting the lines orange instead of regulation blue. Beware what he is saying. Stop thinking about what he is saying and launch into why this is not possible. Shut him down. Now."

Preparation for presenting ideas is so important that we devote Chapter 5 to this topic.

Don't Scare People

One of my best friends at the CIA alerted me when my behavior needed to be toned down. We were both senior managers discussing a new concept: I generated metaphors and analogies that I thought made everything crystal clear but that Peter was at a loss to understand. In a matter of seconds, I was painting a picture of how work could be completely different in five years, while Peter just wanted to know what would be a good first step.

At that point, Peter said, "Carmen, you're really scary when you get like this." He was good-natured and we both laughed. But I also understood that I was overwhelming my audience. From then on, I've been more aware when I cross my passion threshold. I still love metaphors, for example, but I use them more judiciously. I'll stop in the middle of a presentation and ask the audience if they're still with me and if they're OK, acknowledging my intensity and sometimes getting a laugh in the process.

SAY THANK YOU

Lastly, thank people when they are helpful. Recognizing their suggestions—particularly in the company of other people—builds your relationship, acknowledges their status and expertise, and goes a long way in making sure that they leave you alone. Remember, many lifelong inhabitants of the organizational landscape are unlikely to *ever* fully support you. You just don't want them to stop you.

Note

It is unlikely that you can win over all the inhabitants of the organizational landscape, particularly BBBs. Your job is to befriend them so they don't discredit your idea.

In summary:

- Understand what it's like to be them.
- Empathize.
- Ask for advice.
- Have a goal for every conversation.
- Try to find ways to recognize everyone's value.
- Understand the organizational landscape, build supporters, and do the homework to support your idea, including understanding its risks to the organization.

A Radical Idea for Public Sector Rebels

If you plan to make a career in your current organization, I have a bold idea. Consider serving a year or two in a position that will allow you to learn the bureaucratic ropes.

These types of positions are different in each organization: special executive assistants, managers of administrative operations, budget officers, chiefs of staff, or office managers. The learning and nuance you gain from these types of "inner workings" positions will prove invaluable for the rest of your career.

Have You Mastered the Organizational Landscape?

Your work in this chapter is foundational to everything else you will do as a rebel. Work through the questions in Appendix A to assess how well you know your organization. This preparation will make it difficult for others to deny the organizational need for your idea, to discredit the idea's value, or to discount your legitimacy.

Questions to Ponder

- Which influential people in your organization really know how to get a new idea approved and funded? What can you learn from them? How might you get to know them better so that you can learn more from them?

- What kinds of new ideas do people pay attention to in your workplace? What proposals usually get dismissed?

- What is most valued in your organization? Is there a way to link your idea to that?

- What influential BBBs are most likely to resist or discredit your idea? What is most important to these people and how might that affect how they view your proposal? How can you get to know and understand these individuals? How might developing more empathetic relationships with them help you?

- How much time do you spend in meetings with well-meaning benevolent bureaucrats? Are these meetings helping you advance your idea or are you going to them just to be agreeable and a good corporate citizen?
- What might be the three most important things for you to learn about navigating your organizational culture?

5

Communicating Your Ideas

Now that you understand what's important to the organization, have developed good relationships, and have earned credibility, you're ready to take an important next step: presenting your ideas.

Most of us talk about our ideas with passion and enthusiasm, which are essential for getting people's attention. In addition to this positive energy, there are a handful of communications fundamentals to master so that people understand your idea, consider its merits, and lend their support.

Here are some important elements to keep in mind when you are communicating your ideas:[1]

Show what's at stake.
> To get people's attention, frame your idea in terms of what people care about. *Show how the idea relates to what they want.*

Paint a picture of what could be.
> Emotions get people to consider an idea and influence decisions. Paint a picture of how your idea creates a better situation. Expose the gap between how things work today and how they could work. *Make the status quo unappealing.*

Show that the idea can work.
> Highlight what it will take to be successful and where the greatest risks lie. Show the milestones along the way. This demonstrates that you've done your homework and thought through the risks, uncertainties, and practicalities. *People support ideas that they think can work.*

---

[1]. These foundational principles apply any time you're presenting your ideas. If you know that you're going into a controversial meeting, Chapter 6 provides additional details to help you successfully navigate that situation.

Be positive and pithy.
> Show enthusiasm, but don't get so carried away talking that you fail to listen for others' thoughts and ideas. *Keep it short.*

Build support.
> Mobilize people to support the idea. If 10 percent of the people in an organization believe in an idea, it is highly likely to be adopted. *Find your allies.*

Gauge the reaction.
> Listen carefully to the reaction to your ideas. You'll find help in developing next steps. *You need buy-in to proceed.*

Show What's at Stake

If there's nothing at stake—if there are no emotionally compelling risks or rewards for acting on your idea—people will probably ignore it.

Too often, we launch into details about *how* an idea will work before doing the much more important work of communicating *why* it matters so much. Ideas are approved when they're important, when the stakes are high, and when they address the organization's mission, aspirations, or fears.

Emotion is arguably the most potent motivator of human behavior. When issues are important enough, people overcome their apathy or fear to lend their support and get involved. If the issue doesn't affect them in some way emotionally, they are unlikely to risk their reputations or waste their time. When people don't care enough, they often dismiss ideas with statements like these:

- "The timing isn't right."
- "If we're going to do it, we should do it right and we don't have the resources for that right now."
- "I think this needs more study and benchmarking."

At face value, these statements appear factual. Underneath, they really say, "I don't feel the urgency to work toward changing this right now."

So step one is to jolt people awake to express why your idea matters so much *to them.*

Note

The more relevant your idea is to what everyone wants to achieve, the more people will consider it. The more your idea rescues people from a fear or frustration that is getting more acute every day, the more they will consider it. The more widely or deeply felt the issue or topic, the more people will consider it.

If you have tapped into the signals of the organization, you know what's relevant in your workplace. Link your idea to what people are talking about, worrying about, or hoping to achieve.

Examples of "what's at stake" messages range from the risk of losing lives to the frustration of trying to find the damn information for the monthly report, again. The important thing is simply this: does it tug at the emotions of the people whose support you want? Does it provoke them to consider a different approach? Does it tap into pain, frustrations, values, or aspirations that people feel deeply about? Does it inspire them to lend their support?

Position the new idea as integral to what people deeply believe in about the organization—what they want to achieve, be known for, or value. Make it fit within the frame or views that already exist. Examples of existing frames include:

- Cutting unnecessary bureaucracy
- Reducing risk
- Having integrity
- Tapping into the brilliance of our employees
- Creating predictable results
- Easing stress of those on the front lines
- Making us less vulnerable to threats
- Accelerating the transition to a new way of working

Wouldn't It Be Nice?

 When I talked about moving toward a streamlined digital production process at the CIA, no one responded to my description of the future state. When I emphasized the inefficiencies of the current system, using humor to point out wasted and unnecessary steps, everyone in the room perked up. Yes, they had seen that movie too and had always wondered if there might be a better way!

The most common "what's at stake" messages fall into one of six categories (see Table 5-1). Each category lists examples from different types of organizations. Based on your situation, which "what's at stake" message might resonate the most?

Table 5-1. Six common categories of what's at stake messages

Aspirations *Examples:*	Anxieties *Examples:*	Emerging Trends *Examples:*
No patient errors—ever.	If we can't quote the right price, we'll either lose money or customers.	We'll get a two-year lead over competitors if we use this emerging technology.
Freedom from email hell.		
Less hierarchy and bureaucracy.	If our data center goes down, we'll lose $100,000 an hour.	Total transparency is expected; this is a way to show we are transparent.
Spend more time doing work that matters.	Do you want to be grilled by the media on this again?	

Beliefs & values *Examples:*	Status *Examples:*	Autonomy *Examples:*
If we believe in treating women with dignity at our hospital, this is a way to show it.	We'd finally make the "Best Places to Work" list.	If we don't fix this, the boss will start micromanaging us.
	It would be a game changer in our industry.	We can either proactively change our process or risk being subject to more regulations.
Do we want our sales reps out with clients or in the office doing administrative work?	We'd get the recognition needed to launch this globally.	

Note

What matters to the people in your organization? What gets their attention?

Paint a Picture

Now that you've got people's attention and framed the idea, paint a picture of how much better things will be. Make the status quo unappealing and the alternative a much better option, so much better that it is worth the investment to get there. Walk people through how things will work differently with your new approach. Help them *feel* this new way of doing things, evoking a positive emotional response. Remember: people make decisions based on emotions, either the desire to flee from pain or to seek relief and rewards.

Use specific examples to make it feel real:

- "No more pulling your hair out with five types of reports and three different databases to find the information you need."

- "Most customer service calls will be pleasant or at least civil; no more irate people screaming at us on almost every call."

- "We won't need those long Friday budget review meetings because Jack will finally have the reports he's needed for years."

- "No more tedious second guessing and drawn out approval processes with legal."

- "Imagine if you got to work in the morning and only had 20 emails instead of 180."

- "What if we could predict the outcome with 90 percent accuracy?"

Use this kind of evocative frame whenever you talk about your idea, and especially with people who don't like your idea. If they push back, remind them that your idea is about easing suffering or protecting the organization's reputation or making it less vulnerable or defending patient safety. Make it hard to argue against an idea that the organization deeply values. Again, this is why finding out what the organization really values is so important *before* you start communicating your ideas.

Show That the Idea Can Really Work

People support ideas (and people) that they think will be successful. It's vital to show the gap between the ideal and the current state and briefly *highlight* the milestones for closing the gap. Avoid going into detail. If you're explaining, you're losing.

We're sure you've been in the meeting where someone tries to explain exactly how his idea will work. Once you go there, you begin losing momentum and get stuck trying to explain how the sausage will be made—a sausage that no one has ever tasted, a sausage, in fact, that you've never even cooked before.

Developing the essential milestones to get from today to success requires a lot of work. Don't show all the research you've done. If you do, people may get lost in the weeds and start attacking a minor tactical point instead of discussing the strategic value of the idea. Do, however, show that you've done your homework and are not just winging it.

Rebels Without a Clue

 During the first meeting at a company that hired me to help them develop a strategic plan, the CEO told me that he had read up on rebels at work. He said, "I just want to let you know that we squash that kind of person around here."

Curious about why this executive disliked brave souls who bring up new and sometimes uncomfortable ideas, I wanted to understand why the executive was so opposed to rebels.

"I just can't stand it when people throw out big, radical ideas and haven't done any research. You can't just say, 'We should move into this market or expand into this product category.' What are the implications to operations? What kind of sales support will we need? What will it take to hire and train the right people? What will be the impact on cash flow? When might we see a return? One year? Five years? Ten years? I realize you can't have all the answers, but when someone presents an idea they better have done some homework or they'll lose all credibility."

Note

Rebels need to do their homework, be prepared, and understand how to sequence their milestones. Otherwise, their ideas may be quickly dismissed.

People don't support things that they think are unrealistic. The more people believe that the proposed change idea is likely to succeed, the more likely they will support it.

Be Positive and Pithy

How we communicate is as important as what we communicate.

When you embark on your change effort, act as if success is just around the corner. Be cheerful. Be emotional. Show enthusiasm, even if it's not considered cool or professional.

Nothing is less appealing than a dour reformer. Those who oppose you are just waiting for you to lose your cool and your momentum.

On the other hand, don't drone on and on. We've all been to the presentations with flowcharts, timelines, quotes, and charts so detailed you can hardly read them, and a running commentary that never stops for questions. Don't be that person.

Some suggestions to consider:

- Use a photo as a visual metaphor of what's at stake. A tightrope walker. A hummingbird attracted to nectar. A dangerous, dark alleyway. People react, respond to, and remember images.

- Give a brief overview of the value of your idea, no more than 5 or 10 minutes. Then ask people to pair up and write on a piece of paper what would be the same or different at work if the idea were adopted. From this exercise, people begin to see the value of it on their own. You also see new value you hadn't considered.

- Open by telling a fairy tale about the "kingdom," code for your organization. Explain what happens in the story if the knights don't heed the danger. Or what happens when the king eliminates the palace guards. It may sound silly, but stories help you make a convincing argument for change in a novel, engaging way.

Fit Your Idea in a Little Red Wagon

 I'm big on imagery. I like to think of fitting all my ideas into a Radio Flyer. You know what a Radio Flyer is—those red wagons kids pull to carry all their toys. I tell my team that their change proposals should be straightforward and streamlined enough to fit in a Radio Flyer. When I meet with another group to talk about my ideas, I always imagine that I'm pulling my little red wagon behind me.

Build Support

Almost all change starts in small, informal groups of people. Before doing any formal presentations, talk to your rebel alliance about your idea (see Chapter 3 for more about building a rebel alliance).

> *Never doubt that a small group of thoughtful, committed citizens can change the world; indeed it's the only thing that ever has.*

> **— MARGARET MEAD**

Communicating a new idea is a process. It includes developing relationships, learning from others, asking for their help in making the idea better, and enlisting their support to be able to make the idea happen. Rebels often mistakenly think that the way to get an idea approved is to present it to the management team, who will either say yes or no. It's a mistake to focus all your communications efforts on presenting to management. Management doesn't hold all the power.

The way to bring an idea to life is by helping people see the value in the idea for them and asking them to be part of the effort. Socialize your idea with many people, and work hard to get those one or two first followers who will take ownership and start to talk about it with others. The first followers validate both you and your idea. They can often be more influential than those in management.

THE TEN PERCENT RULE

Once the first followers get behind the idea, work together to influence 10 percent of the people in your organization.

Why 10 percent? Scientists at Rensselaer Polytechnic Institute have found that when 10 percent of the people in a group believe in an idea, the majority of the people will adopt their belief.[2]

"When the number of committed opinion holders is below 10 percent, there is no visible progress in the spread of ideas. It would literally take the amount of time comparable to the age of the universe for this size group to reach the majority," says Boleslaw Szymanski, the Claire and Roland Schmitt Distinguished Professor at Rensselaer. "Once that number grows above 10 percent, the idea spreads like flame."

---

2. The findings were published in the July 22, 2011, early online edition of the journal *Physical Review E* in an article titled "Social Consensus Through the Influence of Committed Minorities" (*http://bit.ly/minority_rules*).

If there are 200 people in your organization, you need 20 people behind your idea, willing to say to the powers that be, "We should do this." With just 20 people supporting an idea, it is likely to be adopted. That's not so daunting, is it?

Even if there are 1,000 people in your department or community, 10 percent support means 100 people. You need just 100 people to get leadership's attention, interest others, and get funding for an experiment.

So work on your rebel alliance, not just your PowerPoint presentation. Being a rebel is not about being a hero or lone wolf; it's about creating better ways to work with and for our coworkers. The energy, ideas, and support of a group are much more influential than anything you can do alone, and it is a powerful way to get new ideas adopted.

Communicate as much with those who can help support you as those who hold titles of authority. Talk about ideas at a lunch table in the cafeteria. Invite people out for a beer and pizza to figure out ways to take the idea to the next level. Create a project group and post new ideas and links to helpful articles. Tweet about the idea and learn from people outside your organization.

Note

Your mission is to solve a problem worth solving, not to sell your way to solve it. Be open to new ideas.

By inspiring a tribe of supporters, you can do more to influence those with titles of authority than you could through the greatest presentation you might ever make. When an idea starts to surface in conversations beyond your own, people will take notice, including those in positions of formal authority. And when more than 10 percent of people are talking about what a good idea this might be, managers will likely be ready to listen more intently than they may have before the groundswell started to build.

What if you can't get supporters? It may indicate that your idea is too far ahead of its time.

The Idea Whose Time Has Not Yet Come

If you can't find anyone in the organization who agrees with your ideas, you may need to accept that the time is just not right for your proposal. There is nothing so weak as an idea whose time has not yet come. These words are a corollary to Victor Hugo's observation: "All the forces of the world are not so powerful as an idea whose time has come." Many rebels have told us that they had to wait for years before the timing was right for their idea. If you can't find even one follower among your colleagues, it may be time to go into rebel hibernation. Use that time to evolve your own thinking—there's always that small chance your idea really was lousy.

Gauging the Reaction to Your Ideas

There's one more critical element to communicating, right up there in importance with communicating what's at stake and building a network of supporters: learning how to gauge what people think about your ideas.

A common oversight is not noticing people's reactions after we make a presentation or informally discuss our ideas. We have an opportunity to gain insights into how to build support and improve our ideas every time we talk with someone. Reading the signals will help determine your next move.

When people make eye contact, start to relax, lean in to listen, and nod in agreement, chances are good that they are open to your idea and want to learn more.

Another positive physical signal is laughter. People laugh when an idea is new to them. We laugh when we hear something that disrupts our normal way of thinking. According to Brice Challamel of the creativity consulting company Act One, laughter in a meeting means the audience heard an idea they find disruptive and unusual. Rather than ignoring the laughter (or worse, getting annoyed), rebels should comment on the laughter and ask the audience to explain why they laughed. In a sense, the audience is helping you identify your most rebellious ideas. Welcome that laughter. It means your ideas have potential impact.

If people look quizzical or lean back with their arms crossed and a stern look, they are not with you. When you see this, step out of your agenda to try to understand what the person is wrestling with, and ask some good questions. (Remember: questions are a rebel's best friend.)

You might stop and say, "Jeanne, I sense there's something about this concept that you're not quite sure about." Let Jeanne talk. Do not cut her off or tell her that she's wrong or that she misunderstood your point. You want to listen to determine what your next response or question should be in order to have a helpful conversation for both Jeanne and you.

Here are questions for assessing the response to your idea:

Is the idea clear?

Is the person confused about the concept itself? If so, ask if sharing examples of how another organization is doing this might help to clarify.

Is the issue important?

Perhaps the person understands the idea but may not think it's important enough to spend time on. Ask the person to rate, on a scale of 1 to 10, how important he thinks it is to solve this problem. If the person thinks it's less than 7 in importance, he probably isn't going to be a big supporter.

Are there alternatives?

If the person does think you're tackling an important issue (a 7–10 rating), consider asking, "What other ways do you think we might address this problem?" The "we" implies you're all in it together, and you're focusing the conversation on positive solutions. Your mission is to solve the problem, not sell your way to solve it. If the person suggests new ideas, consider them. Questions and collaboration open up new thinking, which brings in positive, healthy energy.

What are the next steps?

If people have a lot of suggestions when you ask this question, they are engaged. Their responses to how to take it to the next level are a form of buy-in. Conversely, if no one has any suggestions, it may signal that people are not interested or don't think the idea will work.

Would you be willing to help?

This is the ultimate gauge. If people are willing to help, they get your idea, like it, and want to see it succeed. As part of your pre-meeting preparation, think through different ways people can help so that you can get them involved in a meaningful way.

What happens afterward?

One last way to gauge your ideas is noticing what happens *after* presentations or meetings. Do people email positive feedback and additional suggestions? Do they stop you in the hall to say what they liked about the idea or suggest other people to meet with to try to secure funding? If so, you have probably earned their support. Some people are quiet in meetings and prefer to offer comments in a less public way. Take notice.

What If They Don't Like Your Idea?

If you've communicated clearly about how to solve a relevant problem and people don't like your ideas, it's wise to pause and assess whether the issue is important enough to keep going, despite the lukewarm reception.

If no one—not even your most trusted colleagues—think your idea is sound and valuable, that's probably a signal that you should let the idea go or refine it so that people see the value.

If you do have some supporters and you all believe that this change effort is needed, especially at this time, it's time to learn one of the most important rebel lessons of all: how to navigate controversy and conflict, which is covered in Chapter 6.

Questions to Ponder

- What important problem or opportunity does your idea address?

- How will things be different if the idea succeeds? How will people feel as a result of these changes?

- Which what's-at-stake category does your idea fall into? Aspirations? Anxieties? Status? Emerging trend? Beliefs and values? Autonomy?

- Suppose your boss says that she will approve your project today if you can briefly explain the most important milestones on the road to success. Could you respond?

- Who might be most interested in your idea? Who might want to support the idea and get involved? What's the best way to connect with these potential first followers?

- Are you communicating in a positive way that attracts people to your cause? Or are you getting a little too grumpy or intense?

- What signals and cues are most helpful to you in gauging whether people understand, support, or dislike your change ideas?

6

Managing Conflict

There can be no change without conflict. Read that sentence again. It's that important.

Disagreement, controversy, and conflict are the most formidable challenges you'll face as a rebel. There are ways to manage controversy, but there are no ways to avoid it. Great outcomes involve some kind of controversy.

You've no doubt experienced the struggles that go with having unusual and unpopular views. You may have been in a messy, controversial situation and didn't know how to turn it around. The messiness was overwhelming and the stress was horrible. Some of you may even have been in the awful situation of being thrown under the bus when your tireless efforts on behalf of a good idea got you tangled up in a major conflict at work. Good ideas are rarely welcomed without disagreement or controversy.

In this chapter, we'll share some useful ways of minimizing conflict and preparing for it, and tactics to use when it erupts. Of all the chapters in this book, this is the one that we most wish someone had given us when we were starting our careers.

Do You Have to Be Mean to Get Things Done?

 When I was a newly minted senior executive officer in the federal government, I had an opportunity to have a personal coach for about six months. I was excited about the coaching experience, largely because I knew exactly what I wanted help with. I wanted to become more effective. Specifically, I wanted to become *meaner*.

I had done well in my career, but I began to notice that some of the leaders who had reached even higher levels in the organization were very clear-headed about making decisions. I thought that they approached decisions and controversy in a much less sentimental way than I did. While I would worry about how a decision would affect the people involved, other leaders seemed able to make the decision based on what they thought was good for the organization. Although I knew I didn't want to go to the same extremes as some of them, I did think that learning to be meaner was a good growth goal for me as an executive. (I hate to admit that I ever thought this bureaucratically.)

I explained all of this to the coach.

The coach was a wise woman.

"So why are you using the word 'meaner' to describe your goal?"

"Well, I want to make decisions in a less sentimental way, so my shorthand for it is I want to be meaner."

"Hmm...I think that's your problem right there. Do you like mean people?"

"No."

"So as long as you define your goal in terms of becoming mean, I don't think you're ever going to get there. I can see how sometimes you're not perceived to be as serious as you really are, so your ideas don't have the influence they perhaps should have. But what you want to be is more *powerful*, not meaner. You can learn to project more power without becoming meaner. In fact, that's your problem. You think mean and powerful are the same thing."

And although I never did lose my whimsy and sentimentality, I did acquire a few techniques that helped me be more powerful.

Our concern for others and not wanting to be seen as mean are among the key reasons why many of us have such a hard time with conflict. The more skilled we are with conflict, the less afraid of it and the more powerful—or, better yet, influential—we become. Meanness has nothing to do with it.

Types of Conflict: Interpersonal, Structural, and Values-Based

There are several types of conflict in the workplace:

Interpersonal conflict happens because some people just don't get along. They rub each other the wrong way. They get under your skin.

Structural conflicts are inherent in the goals of different organizations. Sales and marketing don't see eye to eye. The engineers don't like the design people. There is strategic conflict. People disagree on the direction the organization should take. And then there is conflict over tactics. People may agree on a strategic direction but can't settle on a tactical approach.

A *conflict of values* is one of the most serious forms of conflict, and it is almost impossible to resolve. If you reflect on situations when you've been unhappy at work and couldn't get along with your boss, you may realize that you had completely different values. You may work for an organization whose values are so different from your own that you just can't make it work. We don't think rebels in these types of situations stand much chance of success. In all likelihood, most of the people in the organization share the same values. The rebel at work is the odd person out.

There is much we can learn about becoming more effective in dealing with interpersonal conflict and structural conflict. The conflict of values, however, is a personal moral dilemma. If your values are far removed from those of your boss or organization, you have a stark choice—suffer at work or leave.

Understand your organization to be able to make change. Create change but don't try to change your organization. If people in your organization hold values that you find intolerable, you won't be able to change them. Trying to do so will wear you out, hurt your reputation, and quite possibly affect important things like friendships and your sense of optimism.

As we address conflict in this chapter, we're talking only about structural and interpersonal conflict.

Note

When you get into interpersonal conflict at work, the best default is empathy. Arguments based on logic lead to an impasse or even more ill feelings.

Three Stages of Conflict

We break conflict into three stages: disagreement, controversy, and conflict itself.

A way to understand these three stages is to look at how strategically important your rebel recommendation is to the organization and how complex the issue is. The more strategically important the topic and the more complex the decision, the more likely it will escalate into conflict. If it's not that important and is relatively easy to resolve, things will likely stay in the less heated, less dangerous disagreement territory. It's important to know where you are—disagreement, controversy, or conflict—because there are different tactics and considerations for each stage.

Here are some of the characteristics of each stage:

Disagreement

Talking about ideas. Differing views and approaches surface, often during routine meetings and casual conversations.

Controversy

Considering new ideas. When disagreements over new ideas lead to the emergence of semi-official positions, controversy emerges. This is a moment of opportunity because people are paying attention to our ideas.

Conflict

Fighting about new ideas. When controversy turns into an issue or a fight, this is conflict. One (or both) sides want to win, and someone will lose. It's the most emotionally fraught stage and where we often face our moment of truth.

Disagreement: Talking About Ideas

Most people aren't comfortable in intense and challenging conversations. What rebels consider interesting conversations others often see as uncomfortable disagreements. When someone suggests having an "open, honest dialogue," we take that person at his word. "Yes, let's have the real conversation at last," we think and jump right in with our views. Before you know it, we're engrossed, asking provocative questions, sharing our observations, questioning assumptions, suggesting alternatives—and quite possibly alienating that person because we're coming on so strong.

So how can we disagree without being disagreeable? Learn from others by really understanding their views? Talk about our different point of view without coming across like we're attacking the other person?

When you're in a meeting or conversation:

Listen before jumping in.

Listen more than you speak, and err on the side of being positive, not combative.

Remember that it's not about winning.

Disagreeing and debating ideas is not about being right; it's about creating understanding and learning. The objective is achieving clarity, not achieving victory.

Take out the emotion.

Open with "Here's what I've observed..." rather than with "I think that..." This takes the personal emotion out of the statement; it's not about you but about the evidence. Inviting people to comment on observations—not you—makes them feel more comfortable expressing their views. You might even try asking questions and making comments without using any pronouns whatsoever (no "I" and no "you"). For example, "What contributed to the situation?" and "What alternatives are there?"

Speak last.

Be the last person to speak at a meeting, and ask a question instead of making a statement. Try it a couple of times to see how it feels. This shows people that you've listened and heard them. The thoughtfulness of your questions shows your understanding of the topic without having to say much. And you might learn something critical.

Good questions are a rebel's friend. They help us learn, research, seed doubt about prevailing assumptions, invite people to consider possibilities, and gauge how much energy exists for creating or resisting change. Unlike statements like "I don't agree with that," questions are less likely to be perceived as oppositional. (Unless, of course, the situation really needs some frank straight talk at that moment.)

When you're leading a meeting:

To assess importance or urgency, ask them to rate it.

How important do you think this issue is on a scale of 1 to 10? Or how valuable do you think that direction would be on a scale of 1 to 10? Asking for a rating helps surface importance. If no one thinks it's all that important, don't waste your energy and reputation capital disagreeing about it.

To keep the conversation positive, frame it in terms of appreciation.

Where has this approach worked well before? What are the upsides of going in this direction? What would success look like to you? What would be the very best outcomes for you? When you engage people with a positive mind-set, they become less defensive and more open-minded.

To focus on possibilities and collaboration, ask, "How might we?"

To move a conversation away from problems associated with your idea, ask a "How Might We" question. *How* implies there's a solution. *Might* makes it safe to suggest ideas that may or may not work. *We* means that we're in this together and are trying to collaborate for the good of the organization.

For example, if someone says the project is too risky to consider, you could ask, "How might we reduce risk and be more daring?" Or, if the resistance is about resources, you could say, "How might we get this new idea off the ground with our existing resources?"

How Might We questions are expansive and inclusive. They breathe fresh air into a stale, tension-filled meeting. They get people back to thinking about possibilities, and out of the negativity of disagreement.

To keep people from feeling defensive, avoid why questions.

Asking why questions during disagreements can make people defensive. *Why* can be seen as interrogating a person, whereas *what* asks about the situation.

Consider the difference between these questions:

- "Why do we always disagree about this issue?"

- "What is it about this issue that evokes such strong emotions?"

The first is about personalities; the second focuses on the issue and puts us on less emotionally volatile ground so that we can have a conversation and work things through.

Disagreement is essential to learning what people think, feel, and want to see happen (or not happen). It can clarify thinking and create shared understanding. Often when there's a difference of opinion, people don't know whether they really disagree, whether they have different information or different values, or whether cognitive bias is coloring their perspective. It's incumbent upon the rebel at work to clarify this for everyone at the meeting. Try to gently surface the reasons behind the disagreement.

We also believe that the most constructive disagreements happen when we're friendly, not defensive, listening for others' ideas and listening to what they have to say without simultaneously thinking about how to rebut their points.

Warning

If you feel yourself getting upset during a disagreement, shut your mouth. Err on the side of saying nothing when you feel like lashing out. The angrier you feel, the quieter you should become. Really. You'll find more on anger and its relationship to conflict later in this chapter.

Let's turn now to controversy, which kicks the potential danger, necessary preparation, and potential for change up a notch.

Controversy: Considering Ideas

If your idea truly challenges the way things have always been done, you will engender controversy. Controversy means people have begun to pay attention and think your idea might be interesting, which is a good thing.

CONTROVERSY IS NECESSARY FOR CHANGE...

Real change often entails controversy. If an idea doesn't generate controversy, it might not be as strong as it could be. If it's really important, some people will disagree with it, if only because they don't yet fully understand it. If everyone agrees on a proposal, is it too similar to what exists? Are you missing an opportunity?

Note

Think of controversy as the necessary mating ritual before various good ideas can give birth to progress.

...BUT THAT DOESN'T MEAN WE LIKE IT

We suspect that some of you are thinking, "I don't like the way this is going. I don't know if I can sign up for controversy and conflict." But you can't run from it. How you handle controversy will determine how your proposals and in fact your entire career will fare. These moments of controversy offer us opportunities to gain new allies, better understand our opponents, and find ways to improve our ideas. They may also provide insight into intractable organizational values that we may never be able to change.

Does Anyone Like Conflict?

I am the poster child for disliking conflict. Luckily, I've had a long-time friend who has helped me understand the value of conflict and of standing up for my ideas when I must. Clark served in government for many years and has a strong rebel streak. He's a truth-telling, full-speed-ahead kind of person. He enjoys a good battle and being at the center of controversy, and he can work that to his advantage. I often wished I had his outlook on controversy, but I don't, although listening to his stories helped me reflect on what I needed to do to get my ideas accepted.

I dive into controversy. That said, I'm always slightly uncomfortable when my ideas are met with silence or people start to change the subject or suggest "tabling the conversation" for later. For many years, I second-guessed myself. Now I notice that people usually come up to me after the meeting to talk about what they were afraid of bringing up in a group and to thank me for being the one to bring up the "real issue." I've finally accepted the value and discomfort of being the one willing to open the can of worms.

No matter where we are on the conflict spectrum, there are some days we would all rather go with the no-controversy proposal, get buy-in, and move on. Resist this temptation. Good ideas need good controversy, and we need good ways to manage it.

HERE'S WHERE YOUR WORK PAYS OFF

When you enter the zone of controversy, you'll see the benefits of all the hard work you did mastering the organizational landscape. If you were thorough, you will have anticipated most of the major points of controversy. If you took shortcuts, you may very well find yourself ambushed by the bureaucracy and outmaneuvered at the conference table.

You'll find a lot of details in this section. That's because in our experience most rebels find themselves in this position and need tactical help and forethought to navigate it well.

Rebel strategies for dealing with controversy build upon many of the same best practices for communicating ideas covered in Chapter 5. Those communication strategies will help you throughout your rebel journey, but navigating controversy will require you to learn some new Jedi moves. Most of the time, we will succeed not through brute rhetoric, but by being better prepared and more mindful than our colleagues.

SOME REBEL DON'TS

As your rebel coaches, we have some ground rules to lay out before we tell you how to prepare for a controversial meeting:

Don't go it alone.

Rebels are always at risk of wearing out their welcome, and we are never more vulnerable than when advocating for controversial ideas. Our colleagues grow tired of just hearing us speak, never mind our ideas. It's a sound strategy to find others who can articulate the change agenda or speak on behalf of our proposals. It makes sense to have these individuals attend key meetings where they can mediate or observe the dynamics more dispassionately than we can.

Don't hide known weaknesses.

We sometimes make the mistake of packaging our ideas in ways that hide known weaknesses. Smart executives love to ask the question we hope will not be asked. Don't go into a meeting with a presentation designed to conceal or avoid points of disagreement; it will come back to bite you. You will lose credibility and trustworthiness, which will hurt your chances of selling your proposal and damage your professional reputation. You will forfeit more than the potential success of your idea.

Don't dismiss objections.

When your colleagues object to your proposals, it means you have engaged them in a significant way. Understand their concerns; don't minimize or dismiss them. Sometimes what really damages us is not so much the controversy but the impression that we don't really understand others' objections. When someone expresses a concern, acknowledge the importance of the point and ask for suggestions in dealing with it. If the person responds, you may have begun the process of turning an opponent or skeptic into a potential ally.

Don't monopolize the meeting.

As a rule, presenting your proposal should take up about one-third of the meeting, and the discussion—which you will guide—should take the other two-thirds. Carefully monitor your share of the conversation time. There is no worse outcome than the "other side" feeling that they did not receive a fair hearing.

Don't focus on the who; focus on the what.

When you wade into controversy, focus the debate on issues, not personalities or value systems. There is nothing to be gained from pointing fingers. When conversations descend into drama, people's minds shut down and they find it difficult to consider ideas and possibilities. So try to stay out of drama.[1]

Don't be absolutist.

Stay away from hard edges. Do not present yourself as the ultimate arbiter of truth. Introduce your ideas with phrases like "What I have observed is," "Have you thought about," or "Here's how I think about it." Statements that are absolutist predict the future with finality. For example, "If we don't make these changes, we will go out of business."

Don't debate the unknowable.

Avoid going down the rathole of debating the unknowable. Some decisions are based on what's known or can be researched. Others, especially innovative ideas, live in the unknowable. By recognizing that something is unknowable, you can get away from debating "what if." You just don't know.

Make sure discussions don't get mired in the "yes it does, no it doesn't" madness that characterizes unproductive arguments.

Don't wing it—ever!

Be prepared by storyboarding the meeting and planning as much as possible in advance.

MAKING CONTROVERSIAL MEETINGS PRODUCTIVE

Your mind-set is half the battle. Being prepared is the other half. Now that we've shared the rebel don'ts, here are success strategies for making controversial meetings as productive as possible.

Be prepared, and get help from allies

Before going into controversial meetings, get together not only with your allies but also with those colleagues who just want to make sure that the meeting is

---

1. We say "try" because it may not be within your power to keep drama down during a meeting. Read the section on conflict later in this chapter even if all you anticipate is controversy.

productive. (These people exist—they can be the secretary to the executive committee or the chief of staff for an important executive.)

Imagine how the conversation might unfold and what kinds of objections or concerns will be raised. Think through how you should handle such objections— not necessarily how to defeat them but how best to explore the issue for the benefit of clarity and progress. And be sure to identify exit ramps so that you avoid ultimatums, unnecessary conflict, and perhaps even defeat. For example, what are you willing to trade or concede for partial progress? What halfway outcome are you willing to accept? How do you prevent the issue from getting kicked upstairs? (Our experience is that this is rarely a good outcome for rebels at work.)

Show the so-what

When you engage in controversy, you will be most successful standing up for structural ideas that support the organization's goals and values. You are advocating *for* positive change that supports what the organization believes is important.

Show what's at stake by framing the idea in terms of what really matters. Show how your idea for change links to a core value, shared belief, or important story at work, such as protecting the organization's reputation for integrity, saving government money, protecting people on the front lines, getting predictable results, or making the organization less vulnerable.

Paint a realistic picture

Paint a realistic picture of what could be. Show that the idea can work. The key verb here is *show*. Once your idea becomes controversial, assertions that it will work are not sufficient or persuasive. Find examples in which others succeeded by overcoming similar obstacles. Focus your examples on the implementation issues. Talk about another organization that successfully navigated uncertainties and obstacles similar to what your organization will face. This will be more meaningful and persuasive to the group than an abstract painting of the beautiful end state you aim to achieve.

On more than one occasion, we've gained credibility by surprising people with practicality. It's important to have ideas that are firmly grounded in reality.

Make the meeting long enough

Make sure the meeting is long enough for what you want to accomplish, but not too long.

If this is the first time you're presenting an idea and it's a big, important idea requiring serious consideration and healthy debate, consider blocking off two to three hours instead of the typical hour-long meeting, which is really only 50 minutes by the time people get settled. A substantive, controversial meeting is a terrible thing to cut short. It takes time to explain your proposal and for people to wrap their minds around the possibilities. You don't want to rush good thinking, especially on a controversial topic.

WHEN YOU ARE IN THE ARENA (AKA THE MEETING)

Now, rebel matador, you are ready to enter the arena with the bulls, the arena we at work call the meeting.

Before you go into the arena, remember that keeping meetings conflict-free is not your goal. If what you're doing is important, people should object and argue with you. The way ahead often has poor signage.

We're too often taught in bureaucracies that conflict in meetings is bad and that we should seek consensus. Remember, consensus is not a decision-making strategy. In fact, it is the opposite. It's a technique to avoid making difficult choices. That said, work hard to make sure the conflict is about the right issues, the ones that really matter.

Note

Building consensus. A stall tactic to avoid making decisions.

Take a deep breath

Before you go into a meeting, take 10 seconds to breathe and decide how you want to show up at (versus in) the meeting, including how you want to feel. Ask yourself: what would the best outcome be? Choose one word as your keyword to recall this vision. Here are some ideas: productive, constructive, intentional, lively—even adventurous.

Explain the focus of the meeting

Start by sharing the intent of the meeting and why it matters. (Even better, put that intent into the agenda you send out with the meeting invitation.) The more controversial the topic, the more important it is to create this clarity. One especially useful technique is to put the graphic shown in Figure 6-1 up in the meeting room.

1. VISION

2. PLANNING

3. DETAIL

4. PROBLEM

5. DRAMA

Figure 6-1. *Use this visual to keep meetings focused on vision (From Quiet Leadership: Six Steps to Transforming Performance at Work by David Rock)*

Explain that the focus of this meeting is to talk about a vision for your particular "what's at stake" issue, so you want to focus the discussion today on vision. Explain that today's meeting is not about planning how to implement the proposal, delving into the details of how it would work, or exploring what could go wrong.

Make a productive statement like the following at the beginning of the meeting: "If I see that we're losing our focus in the meeting, I'm going to step in and get us back on track. We want to make the best use of our time. Does that work for everyone?"

We've never heard of people saying no to this request. When they agree, you've just earned more power and control before the meeting even begins. If people start attacking your proposal and dragging it down into the weeds of detail, drama, or even problems, you can politely point to the visual. Remind the group that everyone agreed to focus on the vision and value of the proposal and suggest a way to get back on track with your agenda.

Establish some ground rules

In addition to agreeing to stay focused on vision, we like to suggest participants agree on ground rules at the start of a session and post them on a wall. Again, people usually appreciate some rules for good conduct, and it helps focus attention on our ideas, not the controversy around the ideas. Some agreements we find useful are:

- Judge ideas, not people.
- Focus on solutions and ways forward; stay away from drama and problems.
- Observations are more useful than opinions.
- Let everyone complete their thoughts; avoid interrupting.
- Ask questions that illuminate, not interrogate.
- Ask questions that are brief and to the point without adding background considerations and rationale, which turn the question into a speech.
- If you want your views to be heard, speak now, not later in backroom side conversations. If the "real" conversations happen after the meeting, it breeds distrust.

After presenting your idea

So now you've presented your idea, including the objections you anticipated. If you followed our guidelines, some two-thirds of the meeting should still be ahead of you. It's time for discussion.

People come to support ideas by discussing them, not from hearing a presentation alone. You want to give everyone time to express their concerns, you want to be able to ask lots of questions to gain clarity, and you want time to end well.

Ask people what they like about the proposed idea immediately after finishing your presentation. When people are in a positive place, they are more open-minded. Help put them in a positive place by asking this question first.

Hear everyone out, acknowledge their points, and reiterate your stand with grace as well as strength. It is wiser to present your view without slamming other people's ideas. Keep your head above the battle. In fact, if you find yourself on the attack, stop immediately. When we attack, we only hurt our reputation, our good ideas, and the credibility and trust we worked so hard to gain.

Ask for participants' advice on how to make the idea work. Ask them what they think the next step for the proposal should be. Trust that other people can come up with solutions, too. Then when you share yours, look for the win-win solution by finding common ground to combine ideas.

Discuss for the purpose of achieving clarity, not to win and score points. Listen to others' points. Respond to them in straightforward ways. Pose interesting questions to your critic: "What frightens you about this issue? What other ways might we be able to address this issue? What in the proposal do you think is worth consideration? Which of the points most concern you?" Ask interesting questions of your supporters as well, such as, "What part of the proposal or situation might be worth zooming into?"

Ending well

To end well, make sure you stop 15 minutes before the meeting is scheduled to end. (We recognize that this is difficult to do, but this is a magical time, not to be short-changed. Some of the most useful insights and real issues come out during this wrap-up.)

Use this time to summarize what people liked about the proposal and their concerns. Then go around the room and ask each person to conclude by briefly sharing one or two comments: "What did you find potentially most valuable about this proposal? What do you think the next step should be?" No one comments on what anyone else says. It's a way of ensuring that all voices are heard—not just the extroverts or negative BBB types—and provides a clear understanding of the whole group's perspectives on the proposal.

One last thought. Pay attention to what's happening as the meeting breaks up. We've both been amazed by the fascinating and useful observations people make when they stand up to leave a meeting. In some cases, the people who have been quiet during the meeting will only speak up at this time. We pay close attention to them when the session ends. In all cases, many appear to feel that they can be more informal and share what they really think when the meeting is officially over.

WHAT YOU'LL GAIN

We can't say that conversations about controversial ideas will always go smoothly (if only!). However, the more prepared you are, the greater the likelihood that you will be heard and that you will learn what is necessary to keep moving your proposal forward. The more prepared, gracious, and respectful you are toward people who don't share your views, the more you establish your reputation as a credible professional to be taken seriously. As rebels, we can spend too much time thinking about our ideas and not enough time planning how to discuss them productively, especially when things get uncomfortable or heated.

By positioning your ideas well and having productive conversations about them:

- You gain agreement and support for taking the next step forward.
- You save yourself from getting embroiled in conflict: the most dangerous, high-stakes playing field.

Conflict: Fighting About Ideas

Being taken seriously during controversy is important. Thinking seriously about the risks of conflict is essential. When issues escalate into conflict, our jobs and reputations are on the line. We need to ask ourselves whether the issue is important enough to continue the fight. The fallout on both professional and personal levels can take a toll.

It is during conflict that we've had friends at work abandon us. People don't want to be "tainted" by being involved in conflict that may not end well. They don't want to risk being seen as our supporters and thus by default supporters of an unpopular issue.

READING THE RIOT ACT

We often become strident during conflict. In fact, the ultimate rebel moment during conflict may come when we decide to read the riot act to the powers that be.

> Warning
>
> The rebel riot act is a last resort, a tactic you hope you don't have to use. Calculate the consequences if it isn't received as you hope it will be.

Steve was so frustrated with the executive team's resistance to new ideas that he finally read them the rebel riot act.

He told the executives that despite all their talk about innovation, managers across the company were stifling innovation. Internal entrepreneurs would continue to leave unless the company changed in some very significant ways. Steve laid out a plan for change, based on research, collaboration with his internal rebel alliance, and exactly what he thought the plan could accomplish.

Reading the riot act to established powers gets attention. It is also risky and requires a lot of credibility. Steve succeeded in getting a rebel innovation pilot funded, but he knows that if he doesn't accomplish his goals in a year, he'll be asked to leave the company.

A wake-up call

The original Riot Act was an English law, enacted by Parliament in 1715. If more than 12 people "tumultuously" assembled and refused to disperse within an hour of a magistrate reading a proclamation, they would be charged as felons. In the last century, "reading the riot act" has become a common expression. It's usually a reprimand or warning to get rowdy characters to stop behaving badly. Reading the riot act is a high-intensity intervention for times when no one seems to be listening.

Rebels read the riot act not because people are rowdy, but because they are complacent. There are times we may need to read the riot act to wake people up to the need for change and to explain that management's refusal to consider alternatives is in fact neglect and is putting the organization at risk.

If an organization has a transparent corporate culture, like Steve's, you are more likely to be able to read the riot act as a way to try to create positive change. Reading the riot act indicates that you care about your organization. You want to help the organization to change and be a part of the change.

Formulating a rebel riot act

A good rebel riot act describes what's at stake and offers a high-level plan to get from today's pain to tomorrow's outcomes. Unlike the "what's at stake" communications approach during controversy, the riot act has a harder bite, a forceful tone, an extremely thorough plan, and a specific call to action. It should include:

- A succinct summary of the problem and its risk to the business. No mincing words.
- Data, or at least several credible anecdotes, to support the point. This can't be viewed as your opinion. You show a pattern that has negative consequences.
- A proposed plan to correct the problem. If you're going to read the rebel riot act, be prepared to ask for what you think can solve the problem.
- Willingness to lead the change, including what you expect to accomplish by when.

WHEN YOU'RE MAD AS HELL

Anger often flares up when we're in conflict. Rebel frustrations can grow so acute that we lash out when our bosses and colleagues least expect it, surprising everyone, especially ourselves. We feel momentarily victorious about saying what needed to be said. The outburst relieves pent-up stress, but then we realize that we have damaged ourselves. People have paid attention to our anger but have not necessarily gotten the point.

When something sets us off, our hearts start racing, our jaws clench, we sweat, our mouths go dry, and the voice in our head barks at us like a drill sergeant, "Set the record straight right this minute, damn it. Don't be a wimp. Give it to them."

In a rage, we attack with our words. We come across as judgmental and hotheaded. When we spew our anger, people run for cover or shut down as they wait for us to finish our rant.

Nothing good comes from these outbursts. Most damaging is that our anger gives others ammunition to discredit us, labeling us as loose cannons, temperamental, hot-headed, immature, unstable, lacking judgment, and maybe even asses. It is all code for implying not so subtly that we are not people the organization can, or should, trust.

What a mess. When you feel you're about to erupt, call on behaviors that help you cool down before spouting off. This requires enormous discipline and much practice. While we have gotten better at this, there are times we still blow up the bridge instead of building it. Anger is such a weakness for so many of us.

Here are some techniques to practice (and they will take practice) to manage anger. When we can learn from and control our anger we're able to act with more credibility, calm, and effectiveness.

No personal attacks

We've mentioned this before when talking about the BBBs and it bears repeating: never attack people, use hurtful or rude language, or belittle them. Personal attacks cut the deepest and are the hardest to recover from. Go after issues, not people.

Look at their side

Try to understand what it's like to be the person (or group) you're angry with. What are they trying to protect? What makes them uncomfortable? What are they afraid of? How people talk about something conveys more information than the words themselves. Listen for the emotion beneath the words. This empathy will help neutralize your anger and help you see more clearly.

Find out what your anger is telling you

Consider the source of your anger a new piece of data to examine. There's something to be understood in why you are angry. Try to observe the real issues. This calms down the negative anger and prevents you from lashing out. You'll glean valuable insights by taking this approach, and you'll earn credibility by showing people that they can express ideas without anyone dismissing them or biting their heads off.

It's not about being right

When we're angry, we often believe we're right and they're wrong. This belief shuts down dialogue. Everyone's views are valid. (Unless some excellent research proves otherwise. If that's the case, show them the data and get onto objective territory as fast as you can.) "Your views are valid. It is risky to change a process that's been in place for years. Similarly, my views are valid too. We face other types of risks if we don't change this process." If you acknowledge others' views, they are more likely to appreciate yours. This sometimes works and sometimes doesn't, especially with BBBs. It's still an approach worth trying.

Acknowledge the tension and disagreement

Disarm the situation by acknowledging that tensions are high and disagreements are real. Here are some tactics:

- We're all feeling frustrated and on edge. Let's go around the room and share what we're feeling in a sentence or a couple of words.
- We're not making progress because emotions are running high. Should we adjourn and cool off?
- Are there data points that might help us see more clearly?
- Should we get someone outside our group to facilitate so that we can resolve this?

These questions recognize the tension and offer an active approach to finding ways to address them. Often people suppress their anger, appearing passive while inside the frustration continues to build, increasing the chances of a harmful emotional outburst when you least expect it.

Quarantine your email and your mouth

Impose a 24-hour no-email, no furious phone call quarantine on yourself. Take a walk or get out of the office. If you're pressed by the other person to respond, say, "I have to reflect on this before being able to respond in a helpful way."

Make a list

Don't think; write. Writing while angry cools you down while capturing potentially valuable ideas. Consider these prompts:

- What are the 10 things that worry people most about this idea?
- What 10 pieces of objective data or anecdotal evidence could help people open up their thinking about this?
- What are 10 things I can do to move the idea ahead that don't require approval or meetings with people who oppose the idea?
- Which 10 people could I talk to who could help me see a way to move ahead?
- What are the 10 worst things that will happen if I abandon this idea?

Anger will always be there

Lastly, accept that anger will always be present and powerful for us. Sometimes we don't realize how much we're invested and are unprepared for the anger that surges within us when things go wrong. We care too much about too much. The secret is being aware of the paradox of anger. It can give power and it can derail it. Use the power, and find ways to stop yourself from doing and saying things that derail your credibility.

Early Warning Signs

 To control my anger, I learned to recognize early warning signs, like that prickling on the back of my neck. I notice my palms getting sweaty and my temperature beginning to rise. As soon as I become aware of the symptoms, I think about what I learned about that ancient center of fear and rage that was the earliest part of the brain to evolve, the lizard brain. Repeating "lizard brain" to myself helps me control my emotions and tame my inner reptile.

As we've said, rebels tend to see possibilities and move ahead faster than most people at work. Helping others see new ways always takes longer than we think it should, and more people, processes, and task forces will try to block us along the way than we ever could envision. Persistence and purposeful patience helps; lashing out and biting their heads off doesn't.

Questions to Ponder

- If you were better at having difficult conversations, what would be different for you at work? What might you be able to accomplish?

- What would help you better deal with controversy and conflict? What two or three practices might be most valuable?

- How might you improve how you guide conversations during controversial meetings so that you achieve your meeting goal? What questions are most useful when you're discussing controversial issues?

- The risks are formidable when you get into the conflict stage. Is your idea worth what's at risk to you? How do you know?

- Have you anticipated the tough questions?

- What helps you control your anger?

7

Dealing with Fear, Uncertainty, and Doubt

In the last few chapters, we've shared a lot of tactical advice. Now it's time to return to the realm of our emotions. Learning to manage our emotions so that they don't manage us may be the most important practice for rebels to learn.

Fear, uncertainty, and doubt can paralyze us. We worry, "If I said or did that I could lose my job. Have I gotten in in over my head? Am I jeopardizing my career?" Part of becoming an effective rebel is looking inside and facing our doubts and fears.

Our emotional journeys as rebels often start the moment we realize that our ideas about what needs to be done don't square with our organization's current direction or the official view of how things work. And the emotional turbulence never really goes away. We know; those are hard truths, but they must be faced.

Some fears might be unfounded and some will carry risk. The challenge is: how can we manage our fears so that they don't stop us from doing the work we know should be done?

A Heretic at the CIA

 I feel very lucky that early on in my rebel journey some-one—a stranger, really—warned me about how emo-tionally difficult it would be. I was at a meeting where government officials and business executives were ex-changing best practices. At the reception afterwards, one of the business executives came to me through the crowd and pulled me aside. Her manner suggested that she had come to the meeting just to give me an important message.

"Carmen, I can tell you're a heretic at the Central Intelligence Agency."

I had never heard the word heretic applied to me. But I have to admit that it resonated as soon as she said it. Was there a flashing neon sign above my head?

"I know you're very uncomfortable in that role," said the executive. "You have to learn to stop fighting the feeling of discomfort. If you don't learn to accept it, you'll destroy your career and maybe your well-being.

"It's not even enough to accept the feeling of discomfort," she continued. "You have to get to the point where you enjoy feeling uncomfortable because that discomfort will reassure you that you're trying to make a difference and being true to your convictions."

I thanked the woman. I never spoke to her again so I don't know why she felt compelled to give me that message. But it was one of the most important pieces of advice I ever received and one that I returned to over and over again. Whenever I was scared as a rebel or frightened about my career, I remembered that was how I was supposed to feel—uncomfortable.

Ten Fears That Can Hold You Back

What fears are holding you back?

Take the quiz in Figure 7-1 to determine whether and to what degree each of these common rebel fears affects you. Working through these questions will help you determine your specific fears and assess whether your assumptions are valid. Don't let an overwhelming yet nonspecific sense of dread hold you back. Be as specific as you can in identifying what may be stopping you and the degree of risk you face.

LOSING YOUR JOB

"I'd love to step up and be more of a rebel at work, but I've got (fill in the blank: a mortgage or a family or college loans) to think about. I can't lose my job." This is the greatest fear for rebels at work.

Here's the deal: few people ever lose their jobs when they're trying to put forward ideas for the good of the organization. We hear people voice this concern all the time, but few are fired for trying to improve things at work. Positive intent helps neutralize negative reactions.

| | Likelihood of happening | | | | | | | | | |
| I'm afraid of... | Highly unlikely | | | | | | | | Highly Likely | |
	1	2	3	4	5	6	7	8	9	10
Losing my job										
Hurting my chances for a promotion										
Upsetting my boss										
Damaging my reputation										
Alienating my colleagues										
Conflict and having to disagree with others										
Looking dumb or not being smart enough										
Having to present my ideas to senior management										
Being made accountable for the entire effort										
Someone else taking credit for my idea										

Figure 7-1. *What are you afraid of?*

The more closely aligned your idea is with what the organization actually cares about, whether it is improving safety or increasing revenue, the less likely you will be fired. If you are viewed as a person who focuses on what's important to the organization and is going the extra mile to develop ideas to accomplish important goals, you will more likely be viewed as a problem solver than as a troublemaker.

Troublemakers get fired; thoughtful fixers are appreciated for earnestness and relevance.

In a recent Canadian survey of the top 10 reasons why employees get fired, issues such as dishonesty, poor performance, and inability to work with others dominated the list. The one reason cited that does resonate with rebel fears of losing their jobs is "refusing to follow directions and orders," what is called insubordination in the military.

Some rebels get fired because they attack people rather than going after policies and approaches that don't work. Be aware that if you attack people personally, they will go after some of your greatest fears: trying to get you fired and publicly questioning your professional competence. It's also important to realize that the greater the risk your idea poses to the organization, the greater the validity of your fear of possibly getting fired.

Takeaways:

Frame your message in terms of what matters to the organization.

Do not practice insubordination.

Focus on achieving progress, not on attacking people.

HURTING YOUR CHANCES OF BEING PROMOTED

The fear of not being promoted can be very real for rebels. Whether rebels get promoted can depend on a number of things, some out of our control and some we can influence.

It's easier with a supportive boss

If at all possible, find a good boss or an influential mentor. It's best to have a boss who values your creativity and isn't threatened by your curiosity, honesty, and passion for developing new approaches. When interviewing for a job, focus as much on the person you'll be working for as the position itself. If you work for a risk-averse boss focused on managing business as usual, your life as a rebel at work will be more challenging. It won't be impossible but it will certainly be more complicated.

Joan was recently promoted because her boss values her creative thinking, frankness, and experimentation with new approaches.

"I'm being promoted to eLearning Director of the college," said Joan. "In a coaching conversation with my boss, she passed on advice from our oh-so-traditional provost, who when hearing I was moving into the position, said, 'She seems to think of herself as a rebel. She will need to let that go as a manager.' I don't plan on drinking that Kool-Aid anytime soon, that's for sure."

Because Joan's boss has her back, she has some breathing room to create new programs and show the value of those programs to the students, provided they stay within the limits of what her boss can approve. If she needs higher-level approvals, her boss may be limited in how much she can help. In this kind of situation, we urge rebels to work as quickly as possible to show results. When you can prove that your ideas provide what the organization values, you build credibility and positively influence the naysayers. Positive results increase your chances of being promoted.

Bosses who support us and coach us on how to navigate work politics are invaluable.

It depends on the organizational culture

Rebels are far more likely to be promoted in organizations that talk about the need for innovation and change. In those cultures, we can position ourselves as innovators or change agents. Just as you want to pick the right boss, it's helpful to pick the right organizational culture. The more future-oriented the organization, the less you have to worry about getting passed over for promotion.

In private industry, the most important indicator of whether you'll get promoted is how directly you influence revenue. If you're a rebel and you're consistently bringing in revenue, the organization is more likely to want to keep and possibly promote you, even if they dislike your rebel ways.

While in grad school, editor Stuart Horwitz worked as an event manager at a swanky Boston hotel. He started changing his look, wearing an earring and a hipster hairstyle, and dressing more like himself than like a Brahmin Boston.

One day the general manager of the hotel walked over to Stuart and gave him a once-over with an expression that clearly conveyed his distaste for Stuart's style. "You bring in the numbers," he said to Stuart and walked off. In other words, while he didn't especially like Stuart, he did like the fact that Stuart's work generated revenue for the hotel.

It bears repeating: the more you contribute to what matters most to the organization, the less you have to fear about losing your job or not being promoted.

It's easier if you engage in good rebel practices

Opportunities for promotion and advancement improve the more we control our emotions, practice good humor, gather supporters, exude optimism, and emulate the many other behaviors of good rebels.

What comes to mind when the organization's leaders hear your name? A troublemaker who's always losing her temper? Or a sometimes misguided but well-intentioned idea person who gets her work done? If it's the latter, you are likely to stay competitive within your peer group. (Of course, we rebels would like to be thought of as the far-sighted visionaries who will save the company, but we must remain realistic.)

One last word about promotions. It would be misleading to suggest that rebels, even the best of us, won't end up losing a few points in our organization's annual performance evaluation rituals. In fact, it's critical to understand that risk and come to terms with it. One of the most difficult emotional roller coasters for rebels occurs when we try simultaneously to be true to our convictions and to remain a high flyer at work. Both of us tried to do that and wound up not achieving either goal very well. By our very nature, we value impact and meaning over more traditional measures of success.

As rebels, some of our change efforts will earn positive recognition. Others will not. The question to ask ourselves is whether the effort provides value to our coworkers and organizations and how much we will learn and grow from taking it on.

Takeaways:

Understand how much support your boss can provide.

Evaluate the receptivity of the organizational culture.

Show positive results as fast as you can.

Be a good rebel.

UPSETTING YOUR BOSS (OR THE POWERS THAT BE)

Even if we're valued performers, the fear of what can happen when we upset our boss or senior managers is real.

When our boss is unhappy with us, it's as bad, sometimes even worse, than fighting with a spouse. The world feels off and we can't relax. We walk on eggshells and obsess over what we can do to get things back to normal. We spend time worrying whether we'll be able to repair the relationship. We begin thinking about whether we should update our resumes, reverting right back to that fear of losing our jobs.

As rebels, we rightly fear upsetting our boss, or our boss's boss. They can make our lives miserable in so many ways.

But how real is our fear of upsetting our boss? Start by considering what most concerns or upsets her and look for ways to avoid those triggers. Most bosses:

- Hate it when we challenge their ideas in front of *their* bosses; they think it makes them look bad

- Want details of our idea spelled out, or to know that we've researched how other companies might be using the idea we're proposing; generalized "big ideas" annoy them

- Hate last-minute surprises and not being forewarned about possible risks

Make it your business to learn what your boss dislikes as well as what he likes. The more you understand what upsets your boss, the more likely you won't do it.

One last point about fearing management. We have found that the more senior the executive, the greater the rebel's fears about upsetting or displeasing that person. Presenting an idea to a middle manager might make you nervous, but presenting that same idea to the executive vice president would make you extremely anxious. Don't be afraid of presenting to senior executives. Remember that they got to where they are by being open to new ideas.

Takeaways:

Make sure you support the bottom line, or whatever results "count."

Understand your boss's red lines and don't cross them.

Invest in learning how your boss likes to receive ideas and feedback.

HURTING YOUR REPUTATION

If I stand up for an idea that is foreign to how we do things around here, will I hurt my reputation? Will I be taken seriously? Will people think I'm a troublemaker? Is the effort worth the potential risk? These fears about our reputations can stop us cold.

John, a rebel manager in a healthcare company, was elated about a new program that his management team had just approved. "This is a 'bet my reputation' kind of an idea," he explained. "If this idea doesn't work, my career at this company will be over."

John didn't need to worry about ruining his professional reputation. He is known as a positive, thoughtful, trustworthy guy who delivers on his promises, and when things don't go as planned, he gives his bosses a heads up as early as possible so that they aren't caught by surprise. He has a track record of introducing and managing successful programs.

Note

The greater your existing reputation capital, such as a history of creating successful programs or managing projects, the less you have to fear about your big rebel idea hurting your reputation.

Some rebels fear being seen as a troublemaker. As we said in Chapter 1, rebels are focused on creating positive change for the organization, not wreaking havoc and destruction as troublemakers do.

But the fear of being seen as a troublemaker may be valid if people in the organization view change and new ideas as "trouble," which they may, and which you have no control over.

One way to evaluate how much your ideas would help or hurt your reputation is to ask yourself (and maybe some trusted friends at work), "On a scale of 1 to 10, 10 being the best, how much would the organization benefit if my idea is successful?" If you answer 8–10, it's likely worth the risk. If it's 4–7, take time to consider it more before charging ahead. And if it's 1–3, it may not be worth it.

One of the questions job interviewers often ask is "What was your biggest failure?" If your idea flames out and you have to look for another job, know that you will have a fascinating story to tell if your idea was in the 8–10 range.

Takeaway:

Remember that everything you say and do will be seen and evaluated in the context of everything else you've said and done. Work on building a positive reputation, which makes for positive context.

ALIENATING COLLEAGUES

Often we have no control over how our coworkers will respond when we are in full rebel mode, working intensely to get something important changed at work.

The fact is that being a rebel is a calculated risk when it comes to how others see us.

We've found supporters and detractors during our careers. Letting the lure of the former and the fear of the latter influence your work is not helpful. It's not predictable and it's ego- rather than mission-driven.

Some people may envy our courage to tread where they wish they could. Others may not like the fact that our ideas would require them to do their work differently. We can't control how others may feel.

What we can do is to stay positive, appreciate and acknowledge our coworkers' ideas and contributions, help others wherever we can, and act with integrity and in the best interest of our organization.

Takeaways:

Build relationships and trust.

Think through what you say and do and how you say and do it, because it will affect others.

Remember that ultimately you cannot predict or control how others will respond to you.

HAVING TO DEAL WITH CONFLICT

We discussed this issue in Chapter 6, but it still deserves a place in any list of the rebel's greatest fears. Fear of conflict stops many rebels from pursuing ideas that could benefit others. Indeed, the desire to avoid conflict or tension of any kind is why the culture of consensus pervades so many organizations today. (And we wonder why organizations aren't changing fast enough or why employees are disengaged.)

This desire inevitably seeps into the workforce as individuals take their cues from the behavior of those in management. Agreement becomes the ultimate good, and disagreements, particularly in public, are criticized as unprofessional.

It is important not to internalize these values. It's absurd for us to censor ourselves just because we know people will likely disagree with us.

What we need to do instead is to reframe conflict as a necessary and potentially fertile part of any change process and handle conflict productively so that we avoid its potentially destructive consequences.

Takeaways:

Recognize that conflict is a necessary and valuable part of any change process.

Do not censor your actions or proposals because people may disagree with them; instead, learn from them and incorporate their ideas to make the ideas better.

Learning how to handle conflict productively is an important rebel skill.

LOOKING STUPID

While the discomfort of engaging in debate and conflict is especially intense, the fear of looking stupid or of not being smart enough also stops many of us from speaking up.

We've both been in situations where we held back, concerned that we might not have the answers and could come across as misinformed troublemakers. But over our long careers we have found that, more often than not, asking a question makes us look smarter. Other people in the room often have the same question but didn't have the courage to ask it.

Raise Your Hand and Speak the Truth

 The guru on the stage was demonstrating his executive coaching approach with an audience volunteer so that the other 800 of us could learn his technique.

I knew little about coaching and was curious. This Ivy League university conference seemed like a good place to learn.

The guru started interrogating the woman on the stage with him, cutting her off before she could fully answer his questions, barking that she wasn't answering his questions, and flippantly responding, "Really? Really?" when she tried to answer the questions.

I couldn't believe the meanness of it all. So I raised my hand.

Mr. Guru took questions from two people before acknowledging me, both people praising his technique and asking softball questions like "Do you use the same approach in phone sessions as in-person sessions?"

I stood up and simply said, "How was that helpful? It seemed intimidating and mean to me."

Silence grabbed the giant hotel ballroom. Even Mr. Guru was at a loss for words.

He glared at me and gave some innocuous response, adding that he'd be happy to speak to me privately later. He then turned to the sea of people and said that this woman, meaning me, was in error. Because we were so far from the stage, we couldn't observe his body language correctly. If we could see better, we would know that the "young lady's" comments were off base. (Calling a middle-aged woman a young lady also made my skin crawl; it seemed so condescending.)

There was a break after the role-modeling session. As I made my way to the refreshments, people came up to me and said, "Thanks for saying what you did. I felt the same way." Conversations ensued, and I would guess that's where some real learning happened.

It's hard to speak up, especially in a huge crowd, especially when you're not a subject matter expert, are early in your career, or are new at an organization.

What if my questions are dumb, we think.

What if they're not?

What if no one speaks up challenging people who treat others meanly, who use professional practices that seem ill-founded, who close down learning and thinking by being smug and sure?

Being a rebel in the workplace rarely looks like reinventing your company, creating new business models, or solving other major challenges. Mostly it's simply being willing to raise our hands and put words to what we and possibly others are feeling, and offering a different way of looking at a situation.

People often look dumb when they don't have all the facts, ask questions not related to the context of the discussion, or complain incessantly. However, if your intentions are positive and you've done some homework, you won't look dumb— just concerned.

Takeaway:

We always count the potential cost of speaking up, especially as a lone voice. Isn't it just as important to count the cost of not doing it?

PRESENTING TO SENIOR MANAGEMENT

Some people say they worry that if they bring up a better way to do things, their boss will say, "Good idea. You go present that to the senior management team." Often this is code for, "I don't want to deal with your idea so I challenge you to present it to the executives and hope that you won't bother."

That dare conjures up our earlier fears about upsetting the powers that be.

Being asked to present your ideas to senior management is a good thing. It's not to be feared, just prepared for. Think of it: this is what you've been waiting for, a chance to present your ideas to people who have the resources and authority to give them life. You are likely the best advocate for your cause. If you're not, ask someone who is expert to provide support.

If your fear is really about public speaking (a fear for about 40 percent of the population), that can be overcome with good preparation and an understanding of what management cares about.

The thing to remember when presenting to senior management is that they don't like long presentations about how your idea will work. Avoid getting bogged down in execution details. We've seen too many rebels lose the interest of leaders by going into long explanations of the problem and exactly how their ideas would solve the problem.

Rather, senior leaders will want you to cut to the chase and address some important questions:

- How does this help us achieve one of our important goals?
- Is it feasible?
- What do you know for sure about the situation and what needs to be learned?
- What are the risks?
- What kind of resources (financial and people) will it take, and is the investment worth the likely outcome?

They may also want to know how long it would take to implement your idea and how you plan to measure progress and success.

Keep the formal part of the presentation short, and leave time for comments. If there are questions and lively discussion about your idea, this signals that they are intrigued and interested. To wrap up a meeting about an intriguing idea, senior leaders are likely to ask you, "What's the next step to assess this idea?" or "What do you need from us to move this idea forward?" Be prepared to answer those questions. They will keep your idea moving and boost your credibility.

One last tip: stay positive. People—at all levels—respond more open-mindedly to positive people intent on helping the organization and the people in it. Senior leaders will actually more clearly hear your idea if you remain positive and focused on the vision of the idea. Whatever you do, never succumb to finger pointing, blame, moaning about problems, or other types of drama. When conversations descend into drama, senior leaders may view you as a whiner rather than a competent person with ideas worth considering.

Tips for overcoming this fear:

- Be prepared.
- Be positive.
- Be brief.
- Be sure to thank them at the end.

NOW GO MAKE THIS HAPPEN

A related concern is, "Gosh, what if managers like my ideas and ask me to implement them?"

This is a valid fear. The good news is that it is almost completely under your control. If you have prepared correctly, researched your ideas, and created the right kinds of alliances in the organization, you can articulate how the idea can best be implemented.

We're reminded of that wonderful scene toward the end of *Finding Nemo* when Gil and his aquarium mates have escaped the dentist's office and are bobbing in the bay in their little individual plastic bags. "Now what?" they ask. As a rebel at work, the ability to think ahead is one of your greatest strategic assets.

You may be asked to run the entire effort, or if you've done your homework, you may be able to suggest a better way to get the job done without you. If implementation isn't your strong suit, partner with someone who is. Create a "hand-off" plan.

Takeaway:

If you are the right person to implement the plan, say thanks for the opportunity. If you're not, come prepared with recommendations about how to move forward.

SOMEONE ELSE TAKING CREDIT

We rebels don't need to run everything or even to be recognized for every idea we have. One of our real values is seeing opportunities and ways to solve problems before other people and signaling for help. As future thinkers, we're like scouts who spot a small brush fire that could turn into a wildfire.

Several successful rebels have told us that one of the best indicators that they're succeeding is that others in the organization start talking about their ideas without giving them proper attribution. We call that a rebel win.

Most rebels are not one-trick ponies. We keep coming up with ideas and often become known as the go-to people for new ideas on how to tackle gnarly problems.

Both of us are much happier letting someone else run with our ideas. Remember the three types of thinkers we mentioned in Chapter 2: future, present, and past? As future thinkers, rebels spot what's coming and create ideas for how to respond to that change. Let the present thinkers figure out how to implement the ideas and manage the projects. That's what they do best, not us.

Takeaway:

Share the credit and know when to pass the baton to others who are ideally suited to making big ideas real. This frees up your energies to uncover the next big thing.

Dealing with the Devils of Self-Doubt

Fear is one thing, but doubt is another. What really stops us is often doubt, which can be like a dense fog, making us feel lost and stuck.

Fears are specific, and once we are aware of them, we can usually find ways to tackle them. Afraid of presenting to senior management? Prepare well, get coaching tips on how they like information presented, practice, and you're on your way to conquering that fear. Afraid you might hurt your reputation? Ask trusted work friends for their views about how solid your reputation is and how much your reputation might be at risk when you stand up for this particular idea.

While fears are specific, doubt is undefined. We've found four techniques that are useful in overcoming doubt:

- Lean on your dominant strength.
- Know your "give-up" line.
- Change your environment.
- Cleanse your assumptions.

LEAN ON YOUR STRENGTHS

When in doubt, look for what has worked for you before. What did you do to move through that earlier storm of doubt? Which of your strengths helped propel you through these periods, and how have you leaned on that strength before to get through a period of doubt?

We all have about five key strengths, according to psychologists Christopher Peterson and Martin Seligman, authors of *Character Strengths and Virtues*. Knowing your strengths helps you push doubt aside and lean on the strengths instead. One way to determine yours is to take the assessments offered at the Authentic Happiness (*https://www.authentichappiness.sas.upenn.edu/*) website. Table 7-1 provides a list of strengths to consider.

Table 7-1. Twenty-four signature strengths[a]

Creativity	Curiosity	Open-mindedness	Love of learning
Perspective	Bravery	Persistence	Integrity
Vitality	Love	Kindness	Social intelligence
Citizenship	Fairness	Leadership	Forgiveness
Humility	Prudence	Self-control	Appreciation of beauty and excellence
Gratitude	Hope	Humor	Spirituality

[a] Source: Christopher Peterson and Martin E. P. Seligman, *Character Strengths and Virtues: A Handbook and Classification* (Oxford: Oxford University Press, 2004).

Lois's dominant strength is her love of learning. When she falls into periods of doubt, she turns to research and learning, which helps her see new ways, test ideas, and jumpstart her confidence. Carmen's is fairness. Another rebel friend's strength is perseverance. When in doubt, he recognizes that if he keeps pushing forward, small step by small step, he is likely to accomplish his goals.

When we're aware of and appreciate what works best for us, we can keep going back to those practices. Most of us, however, get through a self-doubt cycle but don't pay attention to what helped us. Next time, make a note of what helped, because that technique will probably work for you again.

IDENTIFY YOUR "GIVE-UP" LINE

When we are at the end of our rope, we often mutter something under our breath. That's our "give-up" line. The subtext for the give-up line is "I give up" or "I quit." Here are a few give-up lines:

- Gawd, these people are stupid.
- I can't believe I'm wasting my time here.
- I just don't care anymore!

My Give-Up Line

"I just don't care anymore!" That was my give-up line. It took me a long time to recognize it but one day, in a moment of acute self-awareness, I realized that every time I said it (and in fact I repeated it over and over), I would fall into a depression that could last for weeks. From then on, I disciplined myself to hear that line the first time I said it so that I could consciously turn off the emotions that were feeding it. It's amazing how much that one moment of self-awareness has helped me over the years. I still hear myself saying it even to this day, but now it serves as an early warning signal for me to start taking preventive measures —such as a long chat with a good friend or a quick break—to ward off the spiral of self-doubt.

All rebels can benefit from hearing that little articulated outburst of emotion that signals growing frustration and self-doubts. Identify it and get it under control as soon as you can. You may not be able to prevent cycles of self-doubt, but you can shorten them through self-awareness.

CHANGE YOUR ENVIRONMENT

Another practice in times of doubt is to change your environment. Have you ever heard someone say, "What you need is a change of scenery"? There's plenty of wisdom in getting physically or mentally away from what we're obsessing over. Move away from the issue that's drowning you in doubt.

Read a good book. Turn off your devices. Take a walk. Have lunch with someone you enjoy. Meditate. Just get your mind off the nagging rebel problem for a while.

CLEANSE YOUR ASSUMPTIONS

In much the same way that nutritionists urge us to go on mini-fasts to rid our body of toxins, we need to do a mental and emotional cleansing to clear our minds of ideas and habits that are holding us back. What assumptions are blocking you? Which of your deeply held beliefs are in the way? What seeds of doubt are beginning to take root?

Has your idea hardened into an assumption? Is your new idea still relevant? Have you been pushing the same set of "new ideas" for 10 years? Perhaps the reason why you're not getting an audience is that your ideas are no longer new or relevant. This is not an uncommon problem for rebels who become so attached to their original thesis that they forget that even "new ideas" can become old. A good rule of thumb you might find useful: if you're sincerely testing your assumptions, some of them should fail.

Do you lump everyone together by thinking that "no one understands"? Are you ignoring potential supporters because you don't think they would understand your ideas or you think the work they do is not relevant to your goals? One of the most interesting ways to advance a new idea is to start someplace marginal to the larger organization. Starting small or starting stealthy is often a good rebel strategy for building support. There may be supporters you are overlooking; just because people are quiet doesn't mean they're not listening and interested.

A more rigorous approach to driving change, backed by years of research, is to use the Immunity to Change model developed by Drs. Lisa Lahey and Robert Keegan, professors at the Harvard University School of Education and authors of *Immunity to Change: How to Overcome It and Unlock the Potential in You and Your Organization.*

Their straightforward model walks you through what you're unconsciously doing to protect yourself from having to change (the immunity) and helps you pinpoint the deep-seated assumptions that stop you from doing the things that will help you achieve your big goal.

"People rarely realize they hold big assumptions because, quite simply, they accept them as reality. Often formed long ago and seldom, if ever, critically examined, big assumptions are woven into the very fabric of people's existence. But with a little help, most people can call them up fairly easily," say Lahey and Keegan.

We want to assure you that *everyone*, no matter how successful, has fears and doubts. This discomfort is a sign that you're being true to your convictions and doing meaningful work. Fear and doubt can stop you, they can give you energy, or they can just be neutralized. The only thing any of us can really control is how we think. Name and acknowledge your fears, do a little investigating to see how real they are, and then think about the value of what you're trying to accomplish.

And sometimes just pretend that you are a person who can.

Pretend You Can

 When I was in high school I sometimes pretended to be the late actress and writer Ruth Gordon (*http://bit.ly/ ruth_gordon*). At 15, I felt like an outsider and misfit in my big, urban high school. Yet I had drive, confidence, and a hope that things would be different once I got out of that adolescent jail. After performing the role of the prostitute Kitty Duval in William Saroyan's "The Time of Your Life," (*http:// bit.ly/time_of_yr_life*) my sophomore English teacher Mr. Roberts suggested I read Ruth Gordon's rambling autobiography *Myself Among Others*.

Gordon, also a five-foot average-looking girl from Boston, wrote of her determination, perseverance, and "screw them" kind of attitude. The Ruth Gordon line that sang to my young self was, "*A Star is Born* was the movie, but that's fiction. A star is not born, a star makes himself or herself a star." I loved that book. I loved the Ruth Gordon that I had conjured up in my mind. She was a young rebel heroine.

In my freshman year of college I entered a talent contest. Panicking that I had none, I channeled Ruth Gordon and did my Kitty Duval monologue. I won.

Ruth Gordon, a rebel extraordinaire, worked steadily on Broadway and in movies, and then her career took off when she was 70, becoming a star in movies like *Rosemary's Baby* and *Harold and Maude*, and winning an Emmy for her guest appearance on the television show *Taxi*.

Her grit, her vanity, her love of her work (and herself) kept her relevant and thriving.

When she died at 88—still working—the *Los Angeles Times* (*http:// bit.ly/lively_longevity*) wrote:

"Gordon was unique among actresses, not only because she defied the passing of time but because she used it like a bonus, a spiritual annuity paying off....Gordon's salty, uninhibited, sexy, sharp-witted, energetic, convention-snubbing, life-celebrating and joyous assertiveness on the screen obviously reflected what we might call her own soul-set....But she was above all a woman whose whole life, the bruises and the triumphs alike, informed and enriched her performances. She was a life force who became a symbol of the vigorous and even riotous possibilities of the upper years."

So on the days that I need a little rebel push, I pretend to be Ruth Gordon exhibiting all of her joyous assertiveness, and trying to dress as well, too.

And you? Who will you pretend to be so that you can stretch and do the work that only you can do?

Questions to Ponder

- What are the top two fears that hold you back from leading change at work? What can you do to reduce the risks associated with each of these fears?

- What's your give-up line? What is happening around you when you start using it? Now that you know what it is, what can you do differently when you hear yourself start to say it?

- What hidden assumptions might be blocking you from achieving what's especially important at work? How can you test those assumptions to see if they're really true?

- What is your dominant strength? How might you use that strength to increase your confidence?

8

A Guide to Rebel Self-Care

When Jeff was the marketing director at a large automotive parts company, people in the company bristled at his thinking and impatience. His ideas were ahead of most people and appeared risky. What he was proposing was not the way things were done in the industry. At a time when marketing was primarily creative, Jeff was crunching numbers. Was he trying to prove how smart he was? "Arrogant MBA smartass," grumbled many in an effort to discredit him.

Fortunately Jeff reported to a CEO named Mike who, despite his tough-guy persona, was especially astute and insightful about human behavior, including Jeff's. Rather than let Jeff burn out or alienate all his coworkers, Mike suggested that Jeff teach a college course at night so that he could divert his intense rebel energy somewhere else and give the rest of the organization time to catch up with his ideas.

Jeff was one lucky rebel to have a boss like Mike. Most rebels aren't so lucky. We can become obsessive, angry, tired, and ineffective without even realizing it.

In Chapter 7, we mentioned that our fears of getting fired are probably unwarranted. A much more realistic concern is burning out. In this chapter, we look at:

- Heeding the warning signs of burnout
- The three Rs of rebel self-care: retreat, reset, and resiliency
- Knowing when to quit
- Finding the right boss

Don't Let Work Consume You

Although passion for our work motivates us, we can't let it consume our lives. Work is not family, religion, or identity. It's a job. Benjamin Hunnicutt, a historian and professor at the University of Iowa at Iowa City who specializes in the history of work, worries that work is fast replacing religion in providing meaning in people's lives.

"Work has become how we define ourselves," he says. "It is now answering the traditional religious questions: Who am I? How do i find meaning and purpose? Work is no longer just about economics; it's about identity," he says, warning that we are unlikely to find spiritual meaning in work alone.

In other words, love your work *and* live a full life that provides meaning and contributes to your identity. Should things not go well at work, as can happen, you will have better coping skills to bounce back.

We admit that it can be hard to step back or know when it's time to do so. And it's easy to get so wrapped up in your rebel cause that you start to become someone you are not. You forget to be a human.

WORK IS NOT MORE IMPORTANT THAN PEOPLE

Both of us have lived through experiences at work where we neglected to take care of ourselves. They are not our fondest professional memories.

We Need to Get This Project Done Today

 I got up that morning at 3:45 to feed my infant son and drive an hour and a half to my Cambridge office to be in early. The digital marketing agency I managed had a deadline for a big project with a well-known bank. If we could pull this off, I was sure that our reputation would be made and more business would follow.

At 7:30, the phone rang in my office. It was Ellen. Again.

A talented programmer whom I had hired from IBM, Ellen always had some sort of drama going on. She couldn't get to work because her husband's car was broken. (She didn't drive.) Her son was sick. She had to check out a new apartment because her landlord was selling the building she was in. What would it be today?

While the rest of us were the picture of youth and energy, Ellen was not. She was overweight from medications, walked with a cane, and spoke slowly and deliberately while the rest of us acted like crackheads, though our only stimulant was the Internet, with dreams of dot-com glory and big lump sums of money.

"I'm not feeling well this morning," she told me. "I'm at the hospital having a few tests."

"You know we have the bank deadline today," I said, trying to be pleasant.

"I'm pretty sure I'll be in before lunch," Ellen said.

"We'll pay for a cab, Ellen," I said. "We need you to get this project done."

"I know. I'll be there," she reassured me with the genuine hopefulness she always exuded when there was something in her life that prevented her from working.

I tried to be pleasant but I was icy. "OK. Hope you feel better," I said and hung up.

Four hours later, just before lunch, my phone rang.

It was Ellen's husband. She was dead. Ellen had had a heart attack.

Aside from her husband, I had been the last person Ellen talked with and I had acted like kind of a jerk. I felt crushingly sad. I had worried about work and about Ellen being at work. But I had not really worried about Ellen. Who had I become? What was this ambition turning me into?

That humbling day forever shifted my perspective about work. I learned that when you begin to lose your best qualities, particularly those that are most important like compassion and thoughtfulness, you lose yourself.

I resigned four weeks later. I had become someone I didn't want to be.

Heed the Warning Signs

To avoid becoming someone you don't want to be, we suggest you heed signs that indicate you might be reaching an unhealthy breaking point and need a rest.

Here are some external clues that you need a break:

- You view every interaction and opportunity through the lens of your pet project.

- You ask your boss how important your project is on a scale of 1 to 10, and she tells you "maybe 5, no more" and you can't understand it.

- You make your "big idea" part of your performance objectives. When it is rejected as not performance worthy, you fly off the handle.

- Fewer people show up for meetings about your idea, or your idea is put at the end of agendas—or doesn't even make the agenda.

The internal signs, however, are the ones to especially watch:

- You start thinking you're smarter than everyone else in the organization.
- You find yourself arguing with people who are close friends at work.
- You don't recognize yourself when people at work describe you to others. They use words like cynical, negative, or unreasonable.
- You can't hear helpful suggestions from others because you are solely focused on your own agenda.

The most alarming signals come when workmates distance themselves from you and you obsess about work so much at home that your personal relationships become frayed. A rebel with a cause but no love, support, or optimism is unlikely to find meaning at work or at home.

Know, too, that it's difficult to handle the emotional load of being a rebel when there's something else going on in your life. And, of course, there is always something else going on in your life.

When you're in danger of becoming someone you're not or feel crushed by disappointment, manage your anger and frustration, divert your energies into another assignment, take a few weeks off, take deep breaths, go on a vacation, and, for God's sake, don't do anything rash. It's time to invest in some rebel self-care.

The Three Rs of Rebel Self-Care

We suggest three strategies to help you care for your rebel spirit:

Retreating from your cause
Hitting the pause button to give you and your ideas a rest.

Resetting your perspectives
Reevaluating your goals and situation to gain fresh perspectives on next steps.

Restoring your resiliency
Incorporating new habits into your life to increase your resiliency and ability to maintain a positive, balanced mind-set. This may be the most important way for rebels to care for their minds and their souls.

RETREATING: GIVE YOURSELF A BREAK

We often need to hit the pause button to retreat and give our ideas and ourselves a break. It doesn't mean we're abandoning a good idea. In fact, it can be an investment in our idea. Sometimes, as with Jeff, the organization needs time to catch up with our ideas, or we need to let conflict over the issue cool down to the point that useful conversations on next steps can be held.

There's a fine line between advocacy and obsession. When you begin to notice that you've become obsessed and all you talk about is your idea or the problems at work, consider stepping back before you lose credibility and possibly hurt your professional reputation. Notice when your internal tuner warns you that you're becoming someone you're not, snapping at friends, becoming impatient and irritable, not sleeping well. These are all indications that it's time to take a break.

As highly public politicians or entertainers do amid controversy, go quiet for a while. Make time for a vacation. Do work that builds your credibility and doesn't make waves. Hang out with positive people.

A retreat will give you the needed rest to replenish your energy and clarify your next moves. The Irish say that a good laugh and a long sleep are the best cures in the doctor's book. We think they're good cures for a tired or discouraged rebel, too. A tired rebel sees problems; a rested rebel sees possibilities again.

RESETTING: DETERMINE THE NEXT STEP

Retreating gives us the mental space to do some introspection and reset our perspective about what we should or shouldn't do next.

Resetting our perspective is more difficult than continuing on our course of action. Yet the ability to reset and re-envision is important for a rebel's long-term health and effectiveness. As fellow rebel Eric Pennington says, "The dream should never die, but versions of it may need to."

Composer Philip Glass puts it this way: "When I talk to young composers, I tell them, I know that you're all worried about finding your voice. Actually you're going to find your voice. By the time you're 30, you'll find it. But that's not the problem. The problem is getting rid of it. You have to find an engine for change." In other words, how do we ease up on the cause that is starting to define us?

One way is to ask good questions, of ourselves and of people we respect in the organization:

- What's beneath what's going on here?

- What has foiled previous change efforts like this one? What can I learn from those?

- Should I continue to try to advance this idea? What might happen if I let it go?

- What approaches would make a difference in getting this idea back on track?

- Am I making assumptions that just aren't true?

- Who else could help make this idea happen? Who could I talk with to get some fresh perspectives?

Another way to reset is to step back and try to see the bigger picture:

- Was my idea too provocative for a conservative organization? Did I fail to show this conservative organization how the idea would actually minimize risk?

- Was my idea too far ahead of the rest of the organization?

- Did I anticipate how forcefully a BBB would try to stop us?

- Did I show the relevance of the idea to the organization? Was the "what's at stake" compelling enough? Did I get so far down in the weeds of how the idea would work that people couldn't see why it's such a good idea in the first place?

It's natural to want to rehash what happened. The problem is that at some point you begin to get mired in those feelings and think like a victim. It's better to acknowledge the hurt, free yourself of anger and resentment, figure out what you can do to put the issue to rest, and move on. It's not easy but it is essential.

Buddhist spiritual teacher Pema Chödron believes that when things don't go the way we had hoped, it's a test. In her book *When Things Fall Apart*, she says, "When things are shaky and nothing is working, we might realize that this is a very vulnerable and tender place, and that tenderness can go either way. We can shut down and feel resentful or we can touch in on that throbbing quality."

Tenderly accepting a sense of loss *and* being easy on yourself allows us to open our hearts and be ready for what might come next. Maybe it's because we've lived a long time, but we've both found fascinating new professional (and personal) paths emerge from those times that we might have considered "failures."

So be gentle and kind to yourself during a resetting period.

The Involuntary Three-Year Sabbatical

 It was only after I took an involuntary three-year sabbatical from being a rebel that I found a new path and new energy for advancing my change ideas. I was still working at the CIA but because I had burned all the bridges at my previous offices, I joined a new work team and sat among strangers. (Truth be told, it was about the only job I could get.) I made new friends and developed new mentors —including one who had been a rebel earlier in her career and was now a tough manager with a cynical streak and a heart of gold. She too had suffered a difficult loss at work—one that made my own troubles seem insignificant in comparison. Just chatting with her gave me a better perspective on work and armed me with new techniques to navigate the organization.

Being with a new group also allowed me to share my ideas with people who had never heard them before and weren't tired of them. They had a fresh perspective that both encouraged me and prompted some adjustments. At the end of that period, I took a job with responsibilities indirectly related to my reform agenda. I thought that if I proved myself in that position, I would get a chance to start planting the seeds for even bigger change.

And so I did. Sometimes the quickest way to your rebel goals ends up being indirect and circuitous.

RESILIENCY: FIND THE STRENGTH YOU NEED

Resiliency helps us bounce back from setbacks, disappointments, and failures. It's an invaluable asset for everyone in general and rebels in particular. In our experience, three things can help a rebel become more resilient:

- Finding support from like-minded work friends
- Leaning on our biggest strength to remind us of our talents
- Tapping into the optimistic belief that we will be successful, though it may not turn out exactly the way we envisioned it

Finding friends at work

Professional friends can be the best source for optimism and seeing new ways to accomplish ideas. In the 1920s, a group of Oxford University professors felt frustrated and creatively stifled by the academic gravitas of that revered institution. Feeling alienated from the English Department, Professors C.S. Lewis, J.R.R. Tolkien, and other friends started meeting at a local pub every Friday night, calling themselves the Inklings. They were a rebel alliance of sorts.

Their intent, in Tolkien's words, was to explore "vague or half-formed intimations on ideas." These rebels wanted to experiment with new ideas that didn't fit Oxford's view of proper literature. Rather than allowing their frustration to drain them, they came together to share, experiment, and get support. This set them up to create the best work of their careers. For Lewis, it was *The Chronicles of Narnia*. For Tolkien, it was *The Hobbit* and the *Lord of the Rings* trilogy.

They didn't try to change Oxford. Rather, they found a way to create fascinating new work supported by their own rebel tribe while still teaching at Oxford. This approach can serve rebels in their work organizations. Finding people with similar interests, making time to talk about observations and ideas, forming a rebel alliance, and supporting one another in a safe and enjoyable way can replenish our energy and create lasting friendships.

Leaning on our strengths

Another way to move through stressful periods and build resiliency is to lean on the signature strengths mentioned in Chapter 7. Doing so will help you reclaim that strong, positive part of yourself.

Clinical psychologist and resilience specialist Dr. Maria Sirois offers a personal story about how this technique helped her through a stressful period:

One of my core strengths is compassion and, last winter, as our income suddenly became severely reduced, the bills began to pile, and tension in our home mounted. I took out my list, chose one of my gifts—compassion—and spent the next seven days practicing it.

One day, I called a former colleague who had lost her mother and just listened to her grieve. The next day, I wrote a note to my teenage daughter, who I knew was deeply worried. The third day, I visited a local shelter and offered my help. The fourth day, I let a mom with screaming children go ahead of me in line at the supermarket. The fifth day, I spent 10 minutes meditating on self-compassion. The sixth day, I wrote a note to a woman I had read about in our local paper who had just lost an infant son. The seventh day, I took time in the morning to review my acts of compassion and see what had happened. What did I notice? I had more energy, calmness, and clarity about what needed to be done next to help our family get through our crisis.

What had changed externally? Nothing. We were still in difficult straits. What had changed internally? Everything. I had come home to myself in a positive way. I had reminded myself of who I was and what I had to bring to the world—no matter what the world was bringing to me. Who can we become when life pulls the rug out from under us? Our fullest selves, gifted with qualities that enable us to rise. We simply must remember what they are and choose to go toward them.

Generating optimism, a rebel's greatest asset

Appreciating what *is* going well despite everything that isn't is another way to restore our energy and positive outlook. At the end of every day, ask yourself, "What was the one great moment of the day?" Maybe you got a parking spot close to the building on a frigid morning. Perhaps a meeting was canceled, giving you a free hour, or a friend at work said he'd cover a meeting for you so you could get home early to your children. The colors of the early evening sky were brilliant.

It doesn't matter what that great moment is; only that we find time every night to find one. The positive psychology experts say that doing this builds a contagious practice of finding benefits in our lives and of learning to be grateful for what is working.

This practice increases our optimism, and optimism is one of a rebel's greatest assets. It helps us keep going. Persistence and determination are easier to sustain with an optimistic attitude. Being a rebel at work can be stressful, but a positive perspective makes it less exhausting.

Optimists ride the possibility wave to stay motivated. Pessimists show persistence and determination by pushing a rock uphill. People want to surf with you. Pushing heavy objects up steep hills? Not so much.

Optimism can also have a powerful influence on teams at work.

I Think We Can

 I remember my first week on a new job, talking with one of my new teams. Everyone was discouraged and frustrated because the client had told them that he was unhappy with their work.

"Let's try to show the client how much we're accomplishing. What if we change the monthly report formats and list everything that we've accomplished each month in bullet points, right at the top?" I suggested.

"Yeah, right," said Cindy. "What happens if we don't achieve those kinds of results?"

Though I had only been at the agency a couple of weeks, I really believed that the team could achieve more, especially if they tweaked how they did some of the work.

My optimism accomplished two things. The team didn't resist my new rebel ideas, although they were contrary to the way most teams did things at the company, and the team did in fact achieve results that surprised them and the client. Someone genuinely believing that they could succeed lifted the team, and they achieved more than they thought possible.

Science backs up these views on optimism.

Dr. Barbara Fredrickson, a scholar in social and positive psychology and author of *Positivity: Top-Notch Research Reveals the 3-to-1 Ratio That Will Change Your Life*, has found that positivity opens our minds and hearts, making us more creative and receptive to new ideas. Positive emotions also help us to discover new skills, gain new knowledge, and find new ways of doing things—and recover more quickly when things don't go well.

You can't force optimism and positivity. That's why retreating, resetting, and restoring resilience are so important; rebalancing helps us tap into our optimism, which helps us see our next move.

In fact, the subtle difference between positivity and optimism is action, according to Elaine Fox, a psychologist at the University of Essex in England and author of a book on the science of optimism called *Rainy Brain, Sunny Brain*.

"Optimism is not so much about feeling happy, nor necessarily a belief that everything will be fine, but about how we respond when times get tough," she writes. "Optimists tend to keep going, even when it seems as if the whole world is against them."

Note

Optimism lifts. Skepticism requires climbing.

Knowing When to Quit

Sometimes, despite the Three Rs, we may still have to quit. You may need to give up on the idea or possibly leave the organization. We rebels often think we can change people and help organizations to see the light and appreciate our ideas if we just keep at it, try a new strategy, ramp up our networking, rename the program, find new executive sponsors, adjust the budget, or punch up the benefits. Often, that is magical thinking.

Note

Three Rs. Strategies for rebel self-care: retreating, resetting, and restoring resiliency. Retreating from your cause to give you and your idea a rest, resetting to gain fresh perspectives on next steps, and restoring resiliency to regain a positive, balanced mind-set.

GIVING UP ON YOUR IDEA

Sometimes we're blind because we love our idea so much. We're like people in a bad relationship; our friends can see that our lover has dumped us and moved on. They tell us that it's over, yet we cling to some odd hope that it might still work out.

Similarly, we have seen too many rebels, including us, hang on at work when there's no chance our idea will succeed.

People at work might just hate your idea or they may be completely indifferent to it. You don't want to ruin your career by hanging onto an idea that no one cares about. If you hang on too long to a dead idea, people will begin to see you as a problem person instead of a creative person who knows how to come up with great ideas. They will begin to dislike a good idea because they dislike you. As the saying goes, "When your horse dies, get off."

Even if this is the greatest idea you've ever developed, know that there will be more great ideas. Creativity doesn't stop. It's a renewable resource for rebels if we take care of ourselves and build the Three Rs into our lives.

Note
Creativity is a renewable resource if we take care of ourselves.

LEAVING YOUR ORGANIZATION

Here are some signals that may indicate it's time to leave your organization:

- Your values are irreconcilable with those of the organization.

- Your organization is resisting important industry or professional trends. By staying with the organization, you won't keep pace with trends. Becoming irrelevant or outdated is a serious career risk. Leave and go somewhere where learning and being on the forefront of what's emerging is highly valued.

- You have been negatively labeled and are being assigned to projects out of the mainstream mission of the organization, limiting opportunities for growth and learning.

- Frustration and anger have led you to say or do some deeply hurtful things to people, which will be hard to recover from. The tension will make you unhappy and work uncomfortable for quite some time.

- All your mentors and bosses you could work with have left the organization or been assigned far away from your chain of command. You are isolated and unprotected.

- After years of turbulence and attempts at reform, your leadership announces a "back to basics" campaign. The organization has sounded retreat. It will probably be years before the organization is ready to move forward again.

FINDING THE RIGHT BOSS

If you decide to leave, be deliberate in choosing your next position. Here's a list of questions to ask your next potential boss and people in the organization to help you gauge whether it will be a good fit.

What is the organization trying to achieve? How do you measure success?
This question reveals whether a clear organizational purpose exists. When there is a clear purpose, rebels have a much easier time because they can link their ideas to the big organizational goal or purpose. When goals and purposes are fuzzy, rebels can get caught in an unproductive eddy of trying to find solid links with the organization's goals.

What's possible that hasn't yet been done in this [field | company | organization]?
What are the greatest opportunities for the organization?
This question helps you gauge whether the interviewer is a forward-thinking idea person.

What do you especially like about this organization's culture and work environment?
The answer to this question may reveal whether the person is positive and appreciative of the strengths of the organization, or a Debby Downer or Negative Nick consumed by problems and negativity. From our observations, positive, optimistic bosses are more open to—and appreciative of—rebels. (Be sure to sanity-check the answer you receive with other signals from this interview and read between the lines. How long she pauses and what the person doesn't say is as important as what she does say.)

What's the best assignment/project you've ever worked on? What made it so fulfilling?
Does the interviewer enjoy implementation or creating new things? Rebels tend to do better working for a boss who likes creating new things.

How do you deal with failure?
If the organization values experimentation and new ideas, a conversation about failure will be engaging, positive, and specific. This is a good sign for a rebel. If, however, the person hesitates and gives bland, trite answers like "We learn from our failures," dig a little deeper to gauge how comfortable the person really is talking about failure.

How do you support people who question approaches that may no longer be effective and who see alternative ways of doing things?
How a person answers this question is more telling than the words themselves. Is the person comfortable with the question? Does the answer flow easily and

naturally—or does it take a bit to find the words? Does it sound like the person truly values truth-telling idea people? Or do you detect some annoyance? Does the response indicate that people regularly bring up ideas and the boss has a genuine and comfortable way to support those people and ideas?

Take some time to walk around and look around the work environment. Do you sense a lot of energy and positive buzz? Or is there a hushed, disengaged feeling? The environment speaks volumes about whether it's a place rebels can thrive. Are people energetic, laughing, sitting in small groups, and working together? Or is there an eerie, quiet hush with people heads down in their cubicles?

SHOULD I STAY OR SHOULD I GO NOW?

When our values don't line up with our organization's or the culture isn't a good fit, we must assess whether to stay or go. Only you can tell what gives you energy, what depletes your energy, what can be negotiated to make work tolerable, and what is simply intolerable.

Take care of yourself, rebel friends. Learn how to step back, look at your ideas through new lenses, and develop a positive spirit of resilience and optimism.

While innovation and creativity are glamorous concepts, the act of creating change is messy, hard work. It often takes much longer than we think is reasonable.

To succeed, we have to care for ourselves, mentally and spiritually.

Questions to Ponder

- What warning signs tell you that you're in danger of burning out? What is especially important for you to pay attention to?
- What practices might help you become more resilient?
- What questions—and people—could help you assess where you are and the best next steps?
- How will you know it's time to quit?
- What questions will you use to find the right boss? The right organization?

9

Am I Becoming a Bad Rebel?

Each rebel journey is unique. But all unsuccessful journeys—especially when you don't take the time to take care of yourself and maintain your rebel fitness—will look a lot like the rebel arc (Figure 9-1).

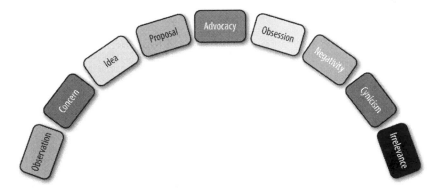

Figure 9-1. *The rebel arc*

You notice something that needs fixing.

You come up with your idea.

You get a hearing, which is fair or less fair. Your ideas don't receive the acclaim you expected. They're just not a priority for the leadership team.

You get frustrated, and then, if you're not careful, slide into obsession.

You don't give up. You can't take no for an answer.

You don't notice how your tone is changing. In fact, many rebels never really understand why people start calling them cynical and negative.

But people at work notice you've changed. They can tell right away. You have slipped into obsession. Next stop—negativity. You've become so pessimistic and angry that people no longer consider your ideas, and you fall into irrelevance.

You are becoming a bad rebel.

Avoiding Bad Rebel Behavior

Most rebels we've talked to admit their behavior sometimes falls on the bad side of the rebel ledger. There are some circumstances in whic such "bad behavior" is unavoidable and even necessary (see "Bad Rebel Doing Good"). But in general, bad rebels cannot survive long in most organizations.

Bad Rebel Doing Good

Is there a place for the "bad" rebel—the person who storms into an organization and bulldozes his change agenda?

Usually, no. But there are exceptions. Like the superintendent of an urban city school system.

Rather than slowly rolling out his change initiatives by building relationships and developing coalitions of support, this educator introduced a dizzying number of reforms and practices in a very short time in what some would say was an autocratic way.

Rather than being humble and patient, introducing change in small bites, he pushed forward big, bold ideas that set off bureaucratic fireworks among school administrators, teachers, parents, unions, and the public.

That he was perceived as an outsider didn't help, either. "He doesn't know how things work in our part of the country," said many of his opponents.

Here's his reasoning for moving so quickly and alienating so many potential supporters:

"Superintendents of large urban school systems have a tenure of about three years—at most," he said. "If I want to have any impact on improving education in this city I need to get as many important initiatives going as possible in the hope that something will stick before I'm asked to leave."

Sure enough, 18 months later there was a shift in politics and he was no longer superintendent.

Did some of his ideas stick? Yes. As much as he would have liked? No.

If we want to create change and keep our jobs, building support and sequencing our change programs is essential. If your position is precarious and the cause important, you may need to move quickly and boldly, trying to get as much "good" adopted as possible, knowing that many will try to block your efforts and discredit your intentions.

Table 1-1, which lists the characteristics of good versus bad rebels, is a useful diagnostic tool for rebels. And if you follow the suggestions we made in Chapter 8 about how to stay fit as a rebel and when to pull over to take a rest, the chances you will stumble into bad-rebel traps are reduced but unfortunately not eliminated. The emotional pressures associated with being a rebel at work are so great that we need all the concrete advice we can get to help us build more productive behaviors. So in the spirit of this handbook, we offer these five practices to follow no matter where you are in your rebel journey. Think of them as a mantra; repeat them often so you don't forget.

1. Play Within the Rules

We can get so disgusted with office politics and bureaucratic nonsense that we start ignoring rules that seem ridiculous. Of course, there is no dearth of rules to ignore; bureaucracies create rules the way urban freeways create traffic jams and pretty much with the same effect.

Breaking rules, like being angry, might give you a momentary surge of "Take that, you idiots." Or, "That really showed them, didn't it?" But deciding unilaterally not to follow certain procedures is a reliable way to be identified as a troublemaker. With that label, you can't gain the maneuvering room and credibility you need to make something important happen.

Creating change at work is a lot like playing chess: The more you understand the rules, the more you can use them to your advantage. Break the rules, and you lose the game. Rebels are in the organization and in the game. If you don't want to work within the rules, get out and create your own organization and rules.

2. Keep Your Sense of Humor

Over the years, we have met way too many humorless rebels at work. Their passion for change has deteriorated into an earnest doggedness that repels people. They respond to any attempt by others to cheer them up by barking, "There's nothing funny about watching this business go down the drain!"

These individuals usually come by their bad humor honestly; they suffered one too many organizational setbacks. Their careers are in disarray and they still can't get anyone to support their ideas. It all seems like such a waste.

It is difficult to regain your sense of humor, so it's helpful for aspiring rebels at work to understand from the get-go the importance of humor and laughter. We think they bring three distinct advantages:

Your sense of humor is an important self-defense mechanism.
This may sound a bit circular, but your ability to laugh at your setbacks and your own mistakes helps you keep a balanced perspective during your rebel journey. It's hard to see the funny side of personal and professional disappointment, which is why it's important for rebels to separate their egos from their ideas. Even if you can't laugh at the time about the dressing down you got from your boss, relax with a friend soon after who can help you appreciate the absurdities. Laughter also has health benefits, and we rebels need to keep our blood pressure under control.

Your sense of humor can win you more supporters.
Writing in *Harvard Business Review*,[1] emotional intelligence expert Daniel Goleman and others argue that an executive's sense of humor is an important business asset. An executive who is happy makes people "optimistic about achieving their goals...and predisposes them to be helpful." You can use humor to lighten the mood of any meeting. You can also use humor to signal receptivity to comments and improvements to your ideas.

Your sense of humor can help you welcome laughter in meetings.
When we take ourselves too seriously, we are all too likely to frame laughter as a form of hostility rather than what it is: an indication that people are surprised by something unexpected. In essence, if someone laughs at your ideas, that person is helping you identify which of your change ideas is potentially most disruptive. We're all familiar with the concept of nervous laughter. People tend to laugh when an idea is completely new. You should be more worried if no one laughs at your ideas.

3. Be an Idea Carrier, Not an Idea Warrior

Beware of thinking that your rebel concept is the one big idea, the silver bullet, or the once-in-a-career opportunity. Remember in Chapter 4 where we talked about the reason so many inhabitants of the organizational landscape resist change? It's because many are trying to keep their one big idea or career-making program or

---

1. Daniel Goleman, Richard Boyatzis, and Annie McKee. "Primal Leadership: The Hidden Driver of Great Performance," *Harvard Business Review* 79:11 (2001): 42–53.

policy alive. We rebels can believe that we own the change agenda in our organizations, and that our experiences and the way we like to do things should become the new orthodoxy. Avoid these behaviors at all costs.

Ideas have their own trajectory. We are the carriers of new ideas; rarely do we "own" them. Just making the mental shift from being an idea owner to an idea carrier can be a game changer. If you are carrying an idea, your number one goal should be to get other people to share the burden—and possibilities—with you. Infect others as soon as you can. Let your idea mutate as it makes contact with other ideas. Make the idea independent of you as soon as you can.

4. Don't Play the Hero

Heroism is not a rebel strategy. Repeat after us. Heroism is not a strategy.

The problem with the ideal of the heroic rebel is that a lone individual is unlikely to triumph over the forces of organizational inertia. Sometimes organizations anoint individuals as saviors, and that usually doesn't work either. The person anointed as the hero is also at considerable risk of believing what people say about him.

Some rebels are probably still storming the ramparts in hopes of overwhelming those who don't get it. In our experience, most organizations become wiser slowly. People start having aha moments here and there. As a rebel, you often have the aha moment sooner than others. If the organization wants to anoint you as a hero for seeing the solution first, resist!

5. Find Your True Rebel Calling

Throughout this book, we've assumed that you have a specific set of ideas for improving the work of your organization. We've suggested tactics and strategies that we think, based on our careers and our research, will give you a better chance of success. All rebels start as advocates of specific changes. But over time, true rebels find a higher calling. The most important evolution your group needs is to become permanently open to new ideas. At that point, your ideas seem less important, and helping advance all good ideas becomes your true calling.

Organizations today are desperate to become more innovative. And we rebels are in a position to help them. If you get off today's innovation bandwagon for a moment, you'll realize that any one innovation in and of itself can't provide the solution. Even if the innovation solves the current problem, it will soon fall behind a new emerging reality. Today's shiny new innovation is doomed to become tomorrow's conventional wisdom.

The issue is not so much whether you are innovative but whether you are *thoughtful* about what you're doing. The issue isn't whether our big idea will happen as much as whether we are helping to create a culture at work where new ideas are considered, discussed, and debated with respect, and given a possible trial. Rebels provide the most value when we help our organizations create thoughtful ways to examine new ideas and identify when it's time to refresh processes and experiment with new approaches. Perhaps the greatest calling for rebels is for us to help organizations evolve from protectors of accepted orthodoxy to discoverers and promoters of new ideas.

Questions to Ponder

- Where are you on the rebel arc? What's your next step to move to—or back to—the center of the arc, advocacy?

- What has happened to you when you've been obsessed about an idea or change proposal?

- How many rebel practices come naturally? Which do you have to work on?

- Do you laugh at yourself? Are you relaxed when you talk to others about your ideas?

- Are you bringing people in to be part of your change initiative? Or are you attempting to be a hero?

- What might your workplace be like if there were a culture where new ideas are thoughtfully considered? What could you and your rebel allies do to create a welcoming culture for new ideas?

10

Give This Chapter to Your Boss

As a rebel, you may want to give this chapter to your boss so that she can better appreciate your value.

As a boss, you may want to understand how to support and lead people in your organization who are constantly trying to change things and introduce new ideas. Then again, you may be a skeptical boss wondering, "Just who are these rebels and what are their motivations?"

Dear Boss,

The first and most important thing to understand about managing a rebel is that this person is not your enemy or even necessarily a troublemaker. In fact, he could be your most valuable employee, helping you identify risks, solve problems, and create better ways to work. The second thing to realize is that many of the young, talented people coming into the workforce think that you want new ideas. They are native rebels who assume that part of their job responsibility is to find ways to improve things at work.

Leaders today talk about the need for more innovative and authentic work environments so that problems can be solved faster, unnecessary bureaucracy trimmed, and opportunities seized. This is exactly what rebels can help you with. It's what they are especially equipped to do, intellectually and temperamentally.

That said, we realize as former managers of rebels ourselves how tiring it can be to supervise someone who constantly generates ideas, asks endless questions, provokes controversy, and occasionally shows frustration and anger that feel uncomfortable or even disruptive.

This chapter helps you understand how to manage a rebel so that you can benefit from her talents and minimize stress. Rebels need bosses who are self-aware, provide concrete support and a safe environment for honest discussions, and serve more as coaches than old-school command-and-control bosses.

We'll talk about:

- What motivates rebels and how they differ from troublemakers
- How to create the right work environment
- What kinds of work to give to rebels
- What kinds of coaching and support rebels need from you so the relationship works for everyone

What Motivates Rebels

To understand how to better manage rebels, it's helpful to understand what makes them tick, their value, and how they differ from whiners and malcontents. The first and most important thing to understand about managing a good rebel is that this person is not a troublemaker (see Table 10-1).

Table 10-1. Bad rebels versus good rebels

Bad rebels	Good rebels
Complain	Create
Assertions	Questions
Me-focused	Mission-focused
Pessimist	Optimist
Anger	Passion
Energy-sapping	Energy-generating
Alienate	Attract
Problems	Possibilities
Vocalize problems	Socialize opportunities
Worry that...	Wonder if...
Point fingers	Pinpoint causes
Obsessed	Reluctant
Lecture	Listen

Rebels will name the elephants in the room, see new ways to solve problems, bring outside ideas into the organization, and be the first to try new approaches. Our research has found that rebels are especially good at pointing out problems and challenging ineffective sacred-cow practices. Both of these qualities are essential to real innovation but are often shunned in organizations.

Rebels also see risks and opportunities sooner than most people. This is a tremendously valuable competence in an age of rapid change, smaller windows to take advantage of opportunities, shrinking budgets, and increased risk of your organization becoming irrelevant.

One way to look at rebels is as "intrapreneurs" bringing entrepreneurial thinking, speed, and competitive instincts into the organization. They spot ideas and see ways to make them real. The challenge is that rebels often move ahead of most people in the organization, and it's difficult for nonrebels to fully understand how the rebel's idea could work given the current realities. One of the jobs of a rebel's manager is to help build bridges from what exists to better solutions, as uncomfortable as those solutions may at first appear to the nonrebels.

REBELS WANT CHANGE THAT REALLY MATTERS

One of the great misperceptions about rebels is that they are trying to change everything or thrive on rocking the boat. Not so. They want to do great work. They want to change things that hold the team back from being its most effective. They are not anarchists. They don't want to reinvent every wheel. They're much too practical to change what's working well.

They do, however, put a lot of effort into eliminating business practices and bureaucratic rules that slow progress without adding value. Bureaucracy creeps slowly. Consensus bloats processes. The "need to know" inflates what needs to be included in standard reports. Legal and quality control "extra safeguards" minimize risk and lengthen the time it takes to get work done. Insecure and inexperienced people add layers instead of revising what exists.

After a while, few people inside the organization can see what's dragging things down or even understand what the regulation or rule means. If they do, they don't know how to fix it. That's where the value of rebels comes in. Unlike troublemakers who rail and rant about how screwed up things are, rebels are often fixers of bureaucracy and unproductive processes. They want to change the rules to reduce the chaos of complexity, creating streamlined order so work can get done faster.

In fact, the mantra of rebel Lars Bjork, CEO of Qlik, is "Love order; hate bureaucracy."

"Order is where you put a process in place because you want to scale the business to a different level," he says. "Bureaucracy is where nobody understands why you do it."

While many people talk about problems at work, rebels recommend possibilities. Whereas troublemakers can become selfish, pessimistic, and obsessed with railing about problems at work, rebels recommend what *can* work, bringing in ideas from outside the organization and remaining optimistic about what can be accomplished.

THEY CARE MORE ABOUT WORK THAN MOST

Did you notice in Table 10-1 that we said rebels *reluctantly* recommend solutions? Most rebels are not motivated by recognition, nor do they want to be viewed as heroes. They simply want to solve problems and improve how things are done, either at a small tactical level or by suggesting wide-scale strategic shifts. They want to make a difference. They have a hard time ignoring a problem that they can see a way to solve. Some find it impossible.

Rebels also care more about their organizations than many people. That's why they're willing to engage in the controversy and conflict necessary for change and to risk being snubbed for unpopular ideas.

A rebel's ideas and relentless energy can exhaust or threaten their colleagues and bosses. People sometimes keep rebels at arm's length, even those who appreciate the value they bring. You may appreciate the rebel's ideas, but not really want to deal with what's needed to create change. Good rebels are not "yes people." They like to really dig into a problem or opportunity, challenging assumptions, asking probing questions, and brainstorming possibilities. Because so many at work like to quickly get to consensus and move on, they sometimes want to avoid a rebel's creative process. (And we wonder why organizations aren't more creative and innovative.)

What Signals Are You Sending to Your Team?

The benefits of helping a rebel succeed are considerable. The consequences of ignoring them are also considerable.

If you consciously or unconsciously shut down rebel thinking, you send a signal to the organization that creativity, diversity of thinking, and change are not welcome. When that happens, your best talent usually leaves and the culture becomes complacent. Few are willing to risk their reputations to rock the boat. The culture accepts good enough as good enough.

In today's hyper-competitive world, how many organizations can survive with a "good enough" culture? How many can survive without the creative thinking needed to solve problems? How can any organization survive without some rebels?

20 Things Never to Say to a Rebel

- You can't.
- You're only doing this because...
- Do what I say and don't ask questions.
- That's the way we've always done it.
- Know your place.
- If you continue to speak your mind, you will ruin your career.
- Be sure to ask permission first.
- That's nice.
- Impossible.
- We have to accept things as they are.
- You can't fight City Hall.
- Because I said so!
- We can't do that!
- Better the devil you know than the devil you don't know.
- That's not how we do things here...
- You need to look more like an executive for people to take you seriously.
- If you rock the boat, you're going to fall out.
- You're too enthusiastic.
- That's enough.
- But the policy says...

Creating the Right Work Environment

Creating a clear organizational vision, making it safe to disagree, and developing organizational habits that keep the culture open to change are the most useful ways to create a productive work environment for rebels (and for everyone else).

BE VERY CLEAR ABOUT SUCCESS

When a rebel clearly understands what the organization is trying to accomplish and why, he can focus his energy on creating ideas that support that goal or vision. Without a clear vision, a rebel may go off in many directions, some helpful and others not so much. It's hit or miss because the rebel doesn't know what success looks like to you. It's important to clarify:

- The organization's core values
- The outcomes you are aiming for
- Where you are trying to go

With this clarity of purpose, the rebel can find better ways to achieve your aspirations. Your role as manager of a rebel is to set the vision, not to tell the rebel to follow a prescribed process or rules to get to that vision (unless, of course, there are significant legal or regulatory risks that could jeopardize the organization if you adopted a different approach). If there is an easier, faster, more rewarding way to get from here to there, why wouldn't you want to consider it?

Your goals may seem crystal clear to you, but don't assume they are to your employees. Rebels frequently lament the absence of clear organizational goals.

Clarity about values and outcomes also becomes the filter through which you and the rebel can evaluate and prioritize. This takes away some of the drama and disagreement over whether you like an idea. The filter is more concrete: "How does this idea help accomplish our goals? How does it improve upon the way we do things today?" Again, rebels express enormous frustration over the fact that their ideas are often dismissed without being evaluated based on sound criteria that align with organizational objectives.

MAKE IT SAFE TO DISAGREE

How you respond to ideas sends a signal to your entire organization about just how safe it is to propose something new. If you provide thoughtful and useful feedback, approve some experiments, and provide people time to further explore a possibility, they will see that you welcome new ideas and that people in your organization can grow professionally by going beyond their job descriptions. Your organization will become known as a place people want to work because it's open to doing things differently and better, and you, the manager, believe that employees are a great source of new ideas. Encouraging talent attracts talent.

The most important aspect of creating a safe environment is often the most difficult thing for a manager to do: make it safe for people to disagree with one another and with you.

Many managers mistakenly believe that a workplace with little disagreement is a healthy workplace. Others just can't stand the uncertainty and disruptive nature of disagreement and controversy. It's unlikely that any meaningful change can happen without controversy. People would rather do what has worked than have to learn something new or admit that a process or program they created is no longer relevant.

Controversy and disagreement are not about fighting, with one side right and the other wrong. It is a process of examining different views, honestly and frankly discussing the possibilities and potential downsides, and learning. Collaboration requires frank conversations and occasional disagreement. Unlike in sports or public debates, there are no winners or losers. There is no right or wrong in disagreeing at work; it's about learning to make the ultimate decision stronger.

Make it safe for people, especially rebels, to disagree with you and others in the organization, to ask provocative questions, and to challenge programs, processes, and even (perhaps especially) your opinions. It's your responsibility to ensure that people feel comfortable asking honest questions and raising genuine concerns. This runs counter to the "strong leader" archetype many of us carry around in our heads, but it is nevertheless essential if you want to ensure that your organization considers all points of view. (This archetype, by the way, provides a convenient excuse for individuals in the workplace not to be more proactive in offering suggestions.)

Meetings are an especially important place to create such an environment. To encourage honest opinions, carve out as much time for questions and conversations in a meeting as you do for the presentation. As the manager, set the tone by asking questions like:

- How would our competitors view this decision? Would they welcome what we have done? How would they try to take advantage of it?

- How else might we solve this problem? Have we let ourselves spend enough time really digging into what might be possible?

- What are we missing?

- What hasn't been said that needs to be said?
- What's one thing we can do to explore this direction?

RELATIONSHIPS, MESSENGERS, AND HEROES

Go out of your way to tell rebels that you're interested in their ideas. Find time to get to know them outside of official occasions that bring you together. Listen without defensiveness. Engage your curiosity. Ask good questions to understand their thinking and share your thinking and experiences. Try to see through a new lens. Tell them what you appreciate about their ideas. Challenge them to take their thinking further and figure out how they might create experiments to test whether the idea would provide the assumed benefit.

And never shoot the messenger, the bearer of reality, the person who is brave enough to tell you the truth. The rebel is your ally and possibly the one person who can save or improve your reputation by alerting you to danger and recommending a new way forward.

Similarly, don't make the rebel a hero no matter how good her ideas or yours.

The problem with the heroic leader or rebel is that there isn't such a thing, at least not for long. An organization incurs considerable risk if it becomes overly dependent on any individual as the wise decision maker. The person anointed as hero is also at considerable risk of believing what people say about him. As former Secretary of Defense Bob Gates once said, "There is something about having great power...that skews people's judgment." Work environments are at risk without sound judgment. Never risk this by getting sucked into hero worship.

BEWARE YOUR BIASES

While managers espouse transparency and employee authenticity, they often judge a rebel's ideas by how he looks or talks. "If only he were more professional and understood how to work in an organization like ours," managers often say, which is code for "It's hard for me to take his ideas seriously." Or simply, "He's not like me."

Take an inventory of your biases. Be fearless when you do, then stay alert to them. (Ask a trusted colleague or two to help you identify your blind spots.)

People should be able to come to work as they are, not trying to look, speak, and use language like everyone else to try to fit in. Effective rebels are both authentic and transparent, sometimes to a fault. They care more about ideas and making a difference at work than they do about creating "the right" impression.

A question to consider: do you inadvertently evaluate people more by their appearance and demeanor than by their ideas?

CREATE ORGANIZATIONAL HABITS THAT ENABLE CHANGE

Another ingredient of creating an effective work environment for a rebel—and perhaps all employees—is to cultivate healthy organizational habits so that change is less disruptive. You might think innovation is about bringing out the next groundbreaking digital device. It's not. It's simply imagining and implementing new, better, more satisfying habits.

How can you as a manager create a culture that adapts to change and even looks for opportunities rather than fights new ideas? Such a culture, in effect, might eliminate the need for rebels.

Consider regularly asking questions that make you and your team think about what you do. During your annual planning process, hit the pause button and set aside time to reflect and discuss things like:

- How do we know when it's time to refresh our processes and doctrine?

- Do we have a review process to help us determine when we need to change something? Who's involved in that process?

- What are the habits of my organization? (One useful definition of innovation is "the opposite of habit.")

- What initiatives have been successful in our organization? What contributed to the success and how can we use those practices again?

- How easy is it for people in our organization to experiment with something new? Is it much easier to keep doing what we've always done? Do individuals in the organization have to be courageous superheroes to experiment?

- Are we creating enough small-scale experiments to test our ideas and learn what does and doesn't work?

- Do we spend more time on problem solving or on imagining what could be possible? What is the right ratio when we are doing our annual planning? Do we let the calendar or a change in leadership dictate our strategic process? Or are we always observing our environment so that we are receptive to new ideas?

- How do we balance the paradox of getting work done with finding new ways to work? Of adhering to standards and processes versus taking risks to get to a better outcome? Of rewarding employee cooperation versus recognizing employees for challenging the status quo?
- What is our process for filtering ideas? Are they helpful filters or blinders?

"Innovation is one of my employer's five key values," an MBA student told us, "but I feel many of the organizational leaders don't embrace it. It's just talk."

Innovation can't be just a word in your mission statement or something that a special task force works on. The climate for new ideas and suggesting ideas needs to be welcoming. Rebels keep telling us, "Management can't just shoot down our ideas if it wants to grow and prosper." They also keep asking questions like, "What can we do when management treats us unprofessionally when all we are trying to do is to protect the company from risk and help it succeed?"

As you look at habits, consider spending some time on empathy, the ability to understand how it feels to work in your organization, and particularly what it feels like being a rebel. Is it a safe climate? Are ideas welcomed or even tolerated? Do employee ideas ever penetrate the middle-management ozone layer? Without this sensitivity, it may be difficult to create an adaptable organization. You may be creating greater organizational risk because some managers aren't allowing new ideas in.

An accurate understanding of organizational realities is a real blind spot for many managers, even those who are very good leaders in other respects.

DON'T EXPECT REBELS TO HAVE ALL THE DETAILS

The final ingredient for creating a safe environment is not to respond to a rebel's idea by asking, "Well, how is the whole thing going to work?" Or worse, "You've got five minutes. Convince me this can work."

This is a real leadership moment for a manager. Don't be the boss whose expectations for neat and orderly change are so delusional that you force your enthusiastic future-thinkers to become hypocrites and package their proposals in slide decks that promise an unrealistic level of certainty. If you demand certainty, you not only will buy into intellectual fraud; you also will eventually tear the heart out of your change champions. We advise rebels to do their homework before presenting their idea and not to conceal its weakness with clever packaging. For your part, ask good questions and explore consequences, but be realistic about how much you can know ahead of time. The real way to test an idea is to experiment with it.

Approach change for what it is—the normal (and messy!) course-correction process that keeps your organization alive. Things externally and internally are constantly changing, and we adjust and adapt in response. Adaptive change keeps organizations healthy, much more so than the big idea, which rarely happens and is often yearned for so that people don't have to do the hard work of constantly adjusting to new realities.

Give Rebels the Right Work

What kinds of work should you give to rebels? We have three recommendations:

- Give them real work.
- Challenge them.
- Put them in key positions.

REAL WORK, NOT INNOVATION TASK FORCES

Don't consign rebels to an isolated innovation lab or assign them to task forces that are not essential to the organization's goals.

Rebels know that being asked to do "rebel work" is a career killer. Most rebels are already distraught at having to choose between speaking their minds and stoking their careers. Rebels often hear in performance appraisal sessions that while their work on such-and-such change initiative was admirable, it distracted them from the organization's mission. Don't make this phenomenon worse by heaping more such assignments on them.

THE THORNIEST PROBLEMS

Assign rebels to your most challenging problems, when your performance as an organization is on the line. Rebels have a keen ability to create clarity from complexity. They excel at creating new ways to solve problems. Give them a concrete challenge, milestones, and deadlines along with the right resources and support. Take your hands off the controls but coach them along the way.

We have found that rebels can stretch farther and achieve more than you or they thought possible. But as their leader, you must give them cover and protect them from the naysayer chorus who will try to resist or even block their ideas. As a rebel leader, you must believe in your people and what they are trying to accomplish.

Be clear about delegating. Make sure you and your colleagues have a shared understanding of the project. We've seen instances in which managers asked a rebel to take on an important organizational assignment and then got cold feet halfway through because the rebel's approach was so novel. The manager started second-guessing the rebel and asking for more frequent and detailed reports and status updates, distracting the rebel from the real work.

Reports are unlikely to allay your fears, and requiring them sends a signal to the rebels that you're not sure they can do the job. Instead of demanding reports, drop in regularly on project meetings and ask direct questions about what's working well and where the group feels stuck or could use help. Unnecessary reports increase unnecessary bureaucracy. Rebels are fighting unnecessary bureaucracy so why heap more on them? Help them with the real work and reduce the busy work.

POSITIONS FOR UNDERSTANDING THE ORGANIZATION

Consider giving the rebel work that will help him understand how the entire organization works. Every organization has key positions that lubricate all the other processes—positions like executive officer or chief of staff. These are usually filled by classic high-performing hard chargers. Try a different approach. Bring someone who is known for having different ideas into these positions. We guarantee the benefits and payoffs will be huge. The rebels will learn to be much more realistic and effective in their approach to change, and the executive team will benefit from a more nuanced and forward-looking perspective.

The Art of Managing Rebels

Effective management is an art. Managing rebels so that everyone benefits requires some specialized approaches to this art.

NO LIP SERVICE

Saying that you support the idea espoused by a rebel is significant, but not significant enough. Everyone in the organization will look to see if you back up your words with actions.

One clear step is to provide money for implementation. In some situations (for example, in most government agencies), shifting resources is not that simple or can only be done at certain times of the year.

Other concrete ways to support rebels include inviting them to present their initiatives at senior leadership meetings and boosting their status and recognition, both of which can be far more desirable than even money. Consider providing funding for them to visit another organization that has created a similar program. By funding such site visits, you convey to them—and others in the organization—that you value their work and want to help them learn all they can.

Five More Things Never to Say to a Rebel

1. Don't you dare.
2. It is what it is.
3. What gives you the authority to ask that question?
4. Yeah, but.
5. You care too much. (Caring is what it is all about.)

BEYOND GENERAL COACHING

The other type of support rebels need from you is coaching. Rebels at different stages in their careers need coaching in different areas. In general, rebels need particular help and guidance in the following areas.

Help them understand the organizational landscape

Few rebels are corporate or bureaucratic natives, so they naively propose ideas without understanding the process for getting ideas adopted. As their coach, help them understand how the system works and why previous reform efforts failed. Suggest that they get to know people who are experts at getting things done in the organization. Guide them on how to roll out a program to build credibility and gain organizational support. Putting things in the wrong order can jeopardize adoption. You know this; they do not. Help them learn the ropes.

Teach rebels to be prepared

Rebels tend to have great instincts and quickly see ways to improve things. Sometimes they promote their ideas too soon and lose credibility. Ask your rebel good questions to help her think through her idea. Help her understand critical research to support her points. Guide her in anticipating resistance and preparing for objections. Learning to build a case is rarely taught in schools, but it is an important skill for rebels. Help rebels learn to build cases for change that can succeed in your workplace.

Show rebels how to present ideas

It's so sad when a person uses the same 50-slide PowerPoint deck about his idea in every meeting. Rebels can fall in love with the details of their proposal and want to go through each and every slide with each and every person who expresses the slightest interest. Save this person from becoming a bore. More important, teach the rebel how to create a presentation or meeting strategy. What does he want people to think after hearing his ideas? What does he need them to do? Based on these goals, what should be presented—and what is unnecessary? The objective is to be to be as succinct as possible. Help the rebel influence opinion, not simply present an idea.

Help rebels use controversy productively

Knowing how to engage in productive controversy and healthy dissent is both an essential leadership and rebel competency. Help them learn how to:

- Show how the benefits of controversial ideas outweigh the risks.
- Ask good questions that elicit helpful input.
- Listen to people and express appreciation for their comments, even if you don't agree with them.
- Disagree without being disagreeable.

If you can coach a rebel on these skills alone, you will make a lasting difference in her career as well as her effectiveness in your organization.

Guide rebels on the next steps

When rebels fall in love with their ideas, they can't see clearly. They have difficulty knowing whether support for their idea is increasing, waning, or just not there. They don't see that they're getting frustrated and angry and alienating people. They can't see that they're exhausted and need a vacation.

As a coach, ask questions to help your rebel find insights about what to do next. Sometimes you may have to be more direct to help rebels know where to stay focused, what to pull away from, and when it's time to let an idea go because the timing isn't right or the idea just isn't going to work. Managers provide much-needed perspective so that a rebel can see the next step. Great managers do this in a way that makes rebels feel appreciated and valued.

Are Rebels Worth the Effort?

People often ask us whether managing a rebel is more work for a manager. Of course it is. Rebels aren't passive order-takers, but most could be considered an organization's high potentials, people who can significantly improve the performance of the organization. And they are not only high potentials in leadership, but in all positions.

Traits of high potentials, according to Cornell University labor management professor Samuel Bacharach, include guts and the courage to take risks amid uncertainty. They'll make tough decisions even if there's a chance they'll fail.

Rebels bring guts and courage in spades. They need you to help them understand how to get to know the organization, how to earn respect from others for their ideas, and how to pace themselves so they don't burn out. Do they require more from you as a manager? Initially, yes. Is the return on your time worth it? Most definitely. They are high performers.

The most surprising value of managing rebels, however, is that they help you grow and become a stronger, more effective leader. A rebel's curiosity, commitment, and passion will inspire you to see new possibilities for your organization and for yourself.

Questions to Ponder

- When you think about rebels, what biases come up for you?
- What might be different if you viewed rebels as allies?
- On a scale of 1 to 10, how safe do people in your organization feel it is to disagree? What could you do to make it safer for people to have honest conversations about issues important to your goals?
- What habits are you developing so that new ideas are not an event, but part of how you and your team work?
- Who are the rebels in your organization? Are they doing the right work?
- What kind of coaching do team members need from you to learn how to sell new ideas to the organization?

Afterword

Rebels are important messengers. We help people see opportunities, emerging trends, and problems. We bridge from what is to what can be.

In Byzantine Greek, the word for messenger is *angelos*, or angel, and in the Bible, angels announced their arrival with the words, "Do not be afraid."

Most of this book has looked at rebels working inside organizations, from companies to government agencies. But rebels are needed everywhere where people are afraid to speak up, from parent–teacher associations to politics to families to nonprofit associations.

People who have stepped out of big organizations to go the free-agent route due to bureaucratic frustration ask us whether it might be possible to re-enter the traditional work world and be effective. "I want to do more than work for myself and make a living. I want to be part of something bigger that has a purpose I believe in."

To these rebels we say, "If an organization's mission is calling to you, go help as the messenger. Use what you've been learning in this book and from the many rebel and change maker communities sprouting up around the world. Bring good ideas forward. Do not be afraid."

In today's unpredictable world, expertise and "solutions" have a short shelf life. The continuous cycle of learning, acting, and adapting needs to be turned from low to high for our organizations to evolve and for us to grow as people.

Crank it up, dear rebels. The world needs us everywhere.

How Well Do You Know Your Organization?

Your success as a rebel in part depends on how well you understand your organization, as described in Chapter 4. If you can answer the following questions, you are well on your way to understanding how to position your idea.

Goals and Vision

How can you show that your rebel idea supports the organization's goals, mission, vision, or values?

- What are the organization's expressed goals or objectives? What goals are most revered—formally or informally?

- What is the organization's philosophy, vision, or purpose? What does it stand for and why does it exist?

- What stories have become legends? What makes the story worth retelling? Are there elements that people would love to recapture? Does the story shine a light on what people really value? Can you make your idea part of this story?

- What does the organization value the most, formally and informally? Risk or certainty? Speed or thorough analysis? Challenging assumptions about thinking or upholding standards? Finding new opportunities or focusing on scaling what exists? What is the organization committed to *not* losing?

Decision Making

What do you need to know about how people make decisions so that you can properly position the idea with people who need to be in the loop?

- Which influential people tend to support what kinds of new programs?

- Who influences whom?

- Who in the organization gets new ideas or projects approved? What helps him get support? Is it the idea? If so, what is appealing about the idea? What is it about his style that helps him move things forward? What could you learn from that?

- How does your boss (or the person you're seeking approval from) like to make decisions? Lots of data and best practices? Knowing that you've socialized the idea with certain key people and received their support? Seeing results from a small-scale experiment? Learning that a competitor is doing something similar? What else?

- How does it feel to be my boss (or any other person you're trying to influence or gain support from)? Given her perspective, what might appeal to her? What is she likely to say no to? What motivates her to take a risk on something new? What holds her back? What new things like this has she approved in the past?

- What are the business cycles? When are new project funding decisions made? How soon in the cycle do new ideas need to be introduced, and in what way? Are initiatives with different sized budgets assessed differently?

- When you ask people to retell memorable stories about work, what kind of words do people use? How might those words help you understand what is most important to people? And, perhaps, frame your idea in language and a story reflective of those that people feel so fondly about?

Assessing Timing

What signs indicate that the time is right for raising your change idea?

- What emerging trend is creeping into conversations? (Is there a way to link with it?)

- What terms and buzzwords are used in the organization that signal that people are looking for new ideas or considering new ideas?

- What types of new ideas have been approved in the past two years? Is there a way to show how your idea is a natural next step to some of the other recent successes?

Handy Rebel Lists

20 Ways to Be a More Effective Rebel

- Be positive.
- Frame it.
- Stay out of drama.
- Judge ideas, not people.
- When angry, stop and wonder why.
- Strive for influence, not power.
- Start the flame; tap into the collective brilliance of others to fuel the fire.
- Share the glory.
- Communicate in ways that create clarity from complexity.
- Address the cost/value tradeoff.
- Let ideas breathe.
- Pick the right boss or executive sponsor.
- Ask good questions; become a keen listener.
- Learn how to facilitate messy collaboration.
- Address the fears.
- Show how success can be measured.
- Learn how to have constructive conversations.
- Be thoughtful in all you do.
- Know when to walk away.
- Believe you are enough.

Top 10 Rebel Mistakes

- Breaking the rules because the rules aren't for you
- Being against the status quo instead of being *for* something
- Skimping on learning the organizational landscape
- Not linking ideas to what the organization *really* values
- Avoiding conflict and controversy
- Putting things in the wrong order
- Wasting opportunities
- Flirting with the dark side
- Going it alone
- Losing your sense of humor

Top 10 Rebel Fears

- Losing my job
- Hurting my chances for a promotion
- Upsetting my boss
- Damaging my reputation
- Alienating my colleagues
- Conflict, having to disagree with others
- Looking dumb or not smart enough
- Someone else taking credit for my idea
- Having to present my idea to management
- Being made accountable for running the entire effort

One-Line Inspirations

On who we are:

> *All you need to know about people is whether they define themselves in terms of their fears of their opportunities.*
>
> **— CARMEN MEDINA**

> *The knowers and seers always live on the outskirts of the village. Always.*
>
> **— PATTI DIGH**

> *They must often change, who would be constant in happiness or wisdom.*
>
> **— CONFUCIUS**

On why we're needed:

> *Impossible is not a fact. It's an opinion. Impossible is not a declaration. It's a dare. Impossible is potential. Impossible is temporary. Impossible is nothing.*
>
> **— MUHAMMAD ALI**

> *We are convinced that any business needs its wild ducks.*
>
> **— THOMAS WATSON**

> *If you're not part of the problem, you can't be part of the solution.*
>
> **— ADAM KAHANE**

About the work:

> *Without grit there is no pearl.*
>
> **— ANONYMOUS**

> *A smooth sea never made a skillful mariner.*
>
> **— ANONYMOUS**

> *A blessing shouted too early in the morning is heard by the neighbors as a curse.*
>
> **— PROVERBS 27:14**

Guidelines for Framing

- Always start with values.[1] Pick a frame where your position exemplifies a value everyone holds—like fairness.

- Never answer a question framed from your opponent's point of view. Always reframe the question to fit your values and your frames.

- Be sincere. Use frames you really believe in, based on values you really hold.

- If you remember nothing else about framing, remember this: Once your frame is accepted into discourse, everything you say is just common sense. Why? Because that's what common sense is: reasoning within a commonplace accepted frame.

Opposition Tactics: The 10 Ds to Try to Stop Your Idea

Here are the 10 Ds that BBBs and others may use to try to stop your idea, courtesy of the Work Group for Community Health and Development (*http://www.commu nityhealth.ku.edu/*) at the University of Kansas:

Deflection

Your opponents may try to deflect you in two different ways. First, they might try to turn the debate to other issues, instead of focusing on the real problem. Alternatively, your opponents may try to "pass the buck" to a group with little or no authority—for example, to a department within their agency, such as the community relations department or to a different organization altogether.

Delay

With delay tactics, the opposition may *say* it is working on the problem, when the reality is that nothing is being done. They may also suggest that more information is needed (and form committees to gather it, as evidence of good faith) when there is already plenty of information on the problem. One of the worst consequences of the delay tactic is that it can hurt the momentum of a strong organization, and it can cause community members to lose heart and give up.

---

1. The guidelines presented here are excerpted from *Don't Think of an Elephant* by George Lakoff.

Denial

Denial is used when your opponent refuses to admit there is any truth to either: a) the problem you say exists or b) the solution that you propose. A second kind of denial is used when officials or other opponents say they would like to help but don't have the resources or clout necessary to actually make a change.

Discounting

Discounting occurs by suggesting that the problem you are working on isn't really that important or by questioning the legitimacy of your organization or its efforts.

Deception

Deception is the act of intentionally misleading someone by lying or by "forgetting" to tell the whole story. Deceptions may be carried out in a variety of ways, such as trying to confuse your organization with bureaucratic nonsense and red tape, misrepresenting statistics, or making suggestions that in reality have nothing to do with what you are trying to accomplish.

Dividing

Opponents may try to divide a group over controversial issues. By doing so, they hope to reduce the overall effectiveness of your organization or coalition. At the most extreme point, opponents may try to "buy off" members with offers of jobs or other incentives.

Dulcifying, or appeasing

To dulcify an organization is to try to appease or pacify members with small, meaningless concessions. This tactic is particularly tricky because it may be difficult to determine the line between compromise (which your group may find helpful) and allowances that turn out to be meaningless.

Discrediting

Discrediting is similar in many ways to discounting. When a member of the opposition tries to discredit an organization, he may attempt to make your group look incompetent (unreasonable, unnecessary, etc.) to the community at large. Your motives and ways of accomplishing your goals are both called into question.

Destroy

The destroy tactic has the simple, clear goal of trying to ruin your organization or initiative in any way possible.

Deal

To "deal" with a group often means to achieve a compromise. In some situations, this can be a major victory for your group. It's important when dealing with the opposition, though, to make sure that what you *get* is equal to what you *give*; this isn't the time to be charitable. Make sure that your group's overarching principles are always foremost in your mind when making a deal with a foe.

50 Reasons Not To Change

Communicating Your Ideas

Show what's at stake.
Show how the idea relates to what they want.

Paint a picture of what could be.
Make the status quo unappealing.

Show that the idea can work.
People support ideas that they think can work.

Be positive and pithy.
Keep it short.

Build support.
If 10 percent of the people in an organization believe in an idea, it is highly likely to be adopted.

When You're Mad as Hell

- Always avoid personal attacks.
- Consider the views of others: what's it like to be them.
- Find out what the anger is telling you.
- It's not about being right.
- Acknowledge tension and disagreement to defuse the situation.
- Quarantine your email, your mouth, your social media rants.

Ways to Avoid Bad Rebel Behavior

- Play within the rules.
- Keep your sense of humor.
- Be an idea carrier rather than an idea warrior.
- Don't play the hero.
- Remember the true rebel calling.

Recommended Rebel Reading

There are so many books that are useful to rebels and that we have found useful. We include here some we've found particularly relevant.

Navigating Inside Organizations

Glenda H. Eoyang and Royce J. Holladay, *Adaptive Action: Leveraging Uncertainty in Your Organization* (Redwood City, CA: Stanford University Press, 2013).

John Hagel III, John Seely Brown, and Lang Davison, *The Power of Pull: How Small Moves, Smartly Made, Can Set Big Things in Motion* (New York: Basic Books, 2012).

Gordon MacKenzie, *Orbiting the Giant Hairball: A Corporate Fool's Guide To Surviving with Grace* (New York: Viking, 1998).

Roger Martin, *The Design of Business: Why Design Thinking Is the Next Competitive Advantage* (Cambridge, MA: Harvard Business Review Press, 2009).

Conflict and Negotiation

Robert Cialdini, *Influence: The Psychology of Persuasion* (New York: HarperBusiness, 2006).

Herb Cohen, *You Can Negotiate Anything* (New York: Bantam, 1982).

Sue Annis Hammond and Andrea Mayfield, *The Thin Book of Naming Elephants: How to Surface Undiscussables for Greater Organizational Success* (Bend, OR: Thin Book Publishing Co., 2004).

William Ury, Roger Fisher, and Bruce Patton, *Getting to Yes: Negotiating Agreement Without Giving In* (New York: Penguin, 2011).

Collaborating

Christina Baldwin and Anna Linnea, *The Circle Way: A Leader in Every Chair* (San Francisco: Berrett-Koehler Publishers, 2010).

David Cooperrider and Diana Whitney, *Appreciative Inquiry: A Positive Revolution in Change* (San Francisco: Berrett-Koehler Publishers, 2005).

Chris Ertel and Lisa Kay Solomon, *Moments of Impact: How to Design Strategic Conversations That Accelerate Change* (New York: Simon & Schuster, 2014).

Patrick Lencionni, *Death by Meeting* (Hoboken, NJ: Jossey-Bass, 2004).

Robyn Stratton-Berkessel, *Appreciative Inquiry for Collaborative Solutions* (Hoboken, NJ: Pfeiffer, 2010).

Communicating

Nancy Duarte, *Resonate: Present Visual Stories that Transform Audiences* (Hoboken, NJ: Wiley, 2010).

Chip Heath and Dan Heath, *Made to Stick: Why Some Ideas Survive and Others Die* (New York: Random House, 2007).

George Lakoff, *Don't Think of an Elephant: Know Your Values and Frame the Debate* (White River Jct., VT: Chelsea Green Publishing, 2004).

Drew Westen, *The Political Brain: The Role of Emotion in Deciding the Fate of the Nation* (New York: Public Affairs, 2008).

Creating

David Bayles and Ted Orland, *Art & Fear: Observations On the Perils (and Rewards) of Artmaking* (Eugene, OR: Image Continuum Press, 2001).

Julia Cameron, *The Artist's Way* (: Putnam, 2002).

Patti Digh, *Creative Is a Verb: If You're Alive You're Creative* (Guilford, CT: Globe Pequot Press, 2010).

Mark Levy, *Accidental Genius: Using Writing to Generate Your Best Ideas, Insight and Content* (San Francisco: Berrett-Koehler Publishers, 2010).

Hugh MacLeod, *Ignore Everybody and 39 Other Keys to Creativity* (New York: Portfolio Hardcover, 2009).

Growing Personally and Professionally

Pema Chodron, *When Things Fall Apart: Heart Advice for Difficult Times* (Boston: Shambhala, 2000).

Elaine Fox, *Rainy Brain, Sunny Brain: How to Retrain Your Brain to Overcome Pessimism and Gain a More Positive Outlook* (New York: Basic Books, 2012).

Barbara Fredrickson, *Positivity: Top-Notch Research Reveals the 3-to-1 Ratio That Will Change Your Life* (New York: Three Rivers Press, 2009).

Seth Godin, *Linchpin* (New York: Portfolio Trade, 2011).

Napoleon Hill, *Think and Grow Rich* (New York: Random House, 2002).

Robert Kegan and Lisa Lahey, *Immunity to Change: How to Overcome It and Unlock the Potential in Yourself and Your Organization* (Cambridge, MA: Harvard Business Review Press, 2009).

David Rock, *Your Brain at Work* (New York: Harper Business, 2009).

Margaret Wheatley, *Turning to One Another: Simple Conversations to Restore Hope to the Future* (San Francisco: Berrett-Koehler Publishers, 2009).

David Whyte, *River Flow: New and Selected Poetry* (Langley, WA: Many Rivers Press, 2012).

Rosamund Stone Zander and Benjamin Zander, *The Art of Possibility* (New York: Penguin, 2002).

Glossary

Accidental rebels

People who are not rebels by nature but are drafted into the role by their boss or by a cause relevant to their family or community.

Adelante

Call to action to move forward with optimism, determination, and joy.

Ass-talking

Ranting about an issue without having done any research or homework into said issue.

Athena trap

The misguided belief that ideas that fix gnarly problems can easily and quickly emerge fully formed without a messy, incremental process. Based on the Greek legend of the goddess Athena springing fully formed from the forehead of Zeus. See Carmen's post on how Obamacare fell into the Athena trap (*http://bit.ly/obamacare_trap*).

Bad rebel

A me-focused individual who breaks rules, is obsessed with change, and alienates potential allies. Bad rebels usually fail, except for brilliant ones such as Steve Jobs, who had the advantage of running his own company. See also "good rebel."

Benevolent bureaucrats

Kinder, gentler bureaucrats. Benevolent bureaucrats emerge when they see a rebel idea becoming a Big Deal with senior leadership and want to be associated with the Big Deal in some way. Because they don't know enough to provide substantive value, they pick on small things to try to insert themselves into the Big Deal, adding unnecessary complexity to the Big Deal.

Building consensus

Stall tactic to avoid making decisions.

Bureaucratic black belts (BBBs)

Individuals who have mastered their organization's rules and culture and know how to enforce those rules, or help a rebel navigate within the rules. Frequently heard to say, "The devil you know is better than the devil you don't." and "There are good reasons why this is the way things are done around here."

Career limiting move

An action or controversial position likely to tarnish a rebel's professional reputation. Despite their best efforts, most rebels make more than one in their career.

Compliant

"Compliant" employees mentally check out of their jobs due to excessive pressure and occasional threats to yield to "the way we do things here."

Controversy

What bureaucrats fear and rebels recognize as a sign their idea is important.

Discretionary energy

Discretionary energy is deployed when people believe deeply in what they are doing and believe that what and how much they do can really make a difference. Group efforts reach excellence when individuals volunteer their discretionary energy to the mission. Discretionary energy is always voluntary. You can never demand it; indeed most managers never know whether someone is giving it their all. Change efforts in organizations live or die based on whether they can evoke discretionary energy.

Discomfort

A chronic condition for rebels who never quite get used to the emotional baggage they have to carry to work for change in their organization.

Flirting with the dark side

The black hole rebels fall into when their only goal is to advance their own agenda.

Get things under control

What BBBs say when they know things are changing; a signal that rebel work is gaining traction.

Give-up line

Articulated outburst of emotion that signals growing rebel frustration.

Good rebel

An individual who operates from a positive perspective, attracts followers, is mission-focused, and is an optimist. Even with all these qualities, still needs to read this book to succeed. (See Bad rebel.)

Heroism

Not a rebel strategy. (See also: Strong hand at the controls.)

Innovation

The opposite of habit.

Lizard brain

The part of the brain where instincts and gut feelings originate. It is also the part of the brain rebels must work hardest to control. When your lizard brain kicks in and spikes your emotions, try to corral it before you say or do something stupid.

Optimism

The ability to continually see possibilities. Optimism is the greatest act of rebellion.

Rebel alliance

Informal group of people who meet at lunch or after hours to support one another in creating change where they work. Inspired by the Rebel Alliance faction in *Star Wars*, which warred throughout the galaxy for the ideals of the Old Republic. Without Darth Vader (and the Emperor), there would have been no need for a Rebel Alliance.

Rebel arc

The stages of a rebel's cause or idea, spanning from observation to irrelevance.

Rebel at work

Sense maker, messenger who sees new ways to create positive changes in the workplace. Synonyms: maverick, heretic, change maker. Antonyms: troublemaker, whiner.

Rebel calling

The desire to help organizations evolve from protectors of accepted orthodoxy to discoverers/promoters of new ideas.

Rebel riot act

When a rebel declares to an assembled group of executives that they are putting the organization at risk by not being open to an important new idea

and calls for the group to seriously consider the idea. Should the assembled group not promptly consider the idea, the rebel declares the probable tumultuous consequences of their inaction. The opposite of The Riot Act established in Britain in 1714. To be used as a last resort, when all other approaches to productive controversy and conflict have failed.

Rebel takeoff point

When your proposal captures the attention of your organization and people are energized negatively or positively. Occurs in the space between advocacy and obsession on the rebel arc.

Rebel win

When a manager likes a rebel's idea enough to steal it.

Strong hand at the controls

Deep human desire to follow someone who will tell us what to do, often leading to hero worship and compliant behavior.

That which refuses to budge

The organization, bureaucracy, status quo at rest, resistant to most attempts at movement.

Three Rs

Strategies for rebel self-care: retreating, resetting, and restoring resiliency. Retreating from your cause to give you and your idea a rest, resetting to gain fresh perspectives on next steps, and restoring resiliency to regain a positive, balanced mind-set.

Way things have always been done
> Code for status quo, and a common response to discredit a rebel's ideas.

Index

We'd like to hear your suggestions for improving our indexes. Send email to index@oreilly.com.

About the Authors

Lois Kelly has been a creative rebel throughout her career, helping some of the most respected companies in the world create new ways to launch products, communicate complicated issues, influence public opinion, deal with crises, go public, adopt innovative business practices, and occasionally try to move mountains.

During this journey, Lois has become a student of change, learning what it takes to get people to embrace new ideas. Her obsession is creating clarity from complexity. Her most meaningful work is facilitating workshops where people create the future they want for their organizations and companies.

In addition to co-authoring *Rebels at Work*, Lois wrote the award-winning *Beyond Buzz: The Next Generation Word of Mouth Marketing*. She tweets under *@LoisKelly*, blogs at *RebelsatWork.com* and *Foghound.com*, and lives in Rhode Island, the smallest and perhaps most creative state in the United States.

Carmen Medina worked at the CIA for 32 years, rising to become one of the highest-ranking women at the Agency.

During her career at the CIA she achieved positions of apparent importance, such as Deputy Director for Intelligence and Director of the Center for the Study of Intelligence (CSI.) But she thinks her greatest achievement is that most people who worked for her are still her friends. She had many ideas about how the CIA could do its job better—not all were welcomed. Being true to yourself, being a rebel at work, Carmen learned, means you will often feel uncomfortable and not welcomed.

Since her retirement from the CIA in 2010, Carmen has continued to write and speak about rebels at work, analysis and strategic warning, the emergence of new global norms in the 21st century, the future culture of work, and cognitive diversity. She is Puerto Rican by birth and Texan by nationality. She tweets as *@milouness* and for *@rebelsatwork* and blogs at *RebelsatWork.com* and *recoveringfed.com*.

Colophon

The cover and body fonts are Scala Pro, the heading font is Benton Sans, and the code font is TheSansMono Condensed.

Have it your way.

Get even more for your money.

Join the O'Reilly Community, and register the O'Reilly books you own. It's free, and you'll get:

- $4.99 ebook upgrade offer
- 40% upgrade offer on O'Reilly print books
- Membership discounts on books and events
- Free lifetime updates to ebooks and videos
- Multiple ebook formats, DRM FREE
- Participation in the O'Reilly community
- Newsletters
- Account management
- 100% Satisfaction Guarantee

Signing up is easy:

1. Go to: oreilly.com/go/register
2. Create an O'Reilly login.
3. Provide your address.
4. Register your books.

Note: English-language books only

To order books online:
oreilly.com/store

For questions about products or an order:
orders@oreilly.com

To sign up to get topic-specific email announcements and/or news about upcoming books, conferences, special offers, and new technologies:
elists@oreilly.com

For technical questions about book content:
booktech@oreilly.com

To submit new book proposals to our editors:
proposals@oreilly.com

O'Reilly books are available in multiple DRM-free ebook formats. For more information:
oreilly.com/ebooks

O'REILLY®

Made in the USA
Middletown, DE
18 July 2020